Come Home to Your Heart

A Guided Journal
for Harnessing Your Inner Wisdom and
Falling Back in Love with Yourself

NADINE KENNEY JOHNSTONE

Copyright © 2023 by Nadine Kenney Johnstone.

All rights reserved. No part of this publication may be reproduced, distributed, or transmitted in any form or by any means, including photocopying, recording, or other electronic or mechanical methods, without the prior written permission of the publisher, except in the case of brief quotations embodied in critical reviews and certain other noncommercial uses permitted by copyright law. For permission requests, write to the author at:

Nadine Kenney Johnstone
Nadinekenneyjohnstone.com

Come Home to Your Heart/Nadine Kenney Johnstone. —1st ed.

Hardcover ISBN 979-8-9875184-1-0

*"I looked in temples, churches, and mosques.
But I found the Divine within my heart."*

R U M I

DEDICATION

For all the women who have desperately been missing themselves.

Welcome home.

CONTENTS

SECTION 1: Looking Within 7

    Chapter 1 Your Inner Sage 9
    Chapter 2 Somebody, Someday 18
    Chapter 3 Put the Paintbrush Down 26
    Chapter 4 Loosen the Edges 34
    Chapter 5 Pay It Forward 41
    Chapter 6 Again 48
    Chapter 7 Remember Today 54

SECTION 2: Learning and Expanding 61

    Chapter 8 Triage 63
    Chapter 9 Try Again Politely 71
    Chapter 10 What Would Barbara Do? 78
    Chapter 11 Nature Lessons 85
    Chapter 12 Witnessing 92
    Chapter 13 Trampoline Savasana 98
    Chapter 14 Noticing Walks 103

SECTION 3: Dealing and Healing When Life Doesn't Go As Planned .. 111

    Chapter 15 Fierce 113
    Chapter 16 Finding Joy in Hidden Places 120
    Chapter 17 Puzzle Pieces 127
    Chapter 18 The Last First Snowfall 135
    Chapter 19 That's Not Your Yard 140
    Chapter 20 The Opposite of Loss 146
    Chapter 21 You Are Welcome Here 153

SECTION 4: Charting a New Course 161

    Chapter 22 The Hum of Your Heart 163
    Chapter 23 Coyotes 169
    Chapter 24 Finding New Shells 176
    Chapter 25 Just Stand Up 182
    Chapter 26 Walks in the Woods 187
    Chapter 27 If You Want to Know Who I Am 194
    Chapter 28 Forever Home 197

Epilogue 203
Resources 205
References. 207
Acknowledgments. 209
About the Author 211

SECTION 1
Looking Within

CHAPTER 1
Your Inner Sage

Take a breath, Sweetheart.
Slow it down, Honey.
It's all going to be OK.

I wrote these words to myself on a summer afternoon in my early 30s when it felt like things were definitely not going to be OK. It was one of those days when everyone else seemed to be skipping on sunshine. I was at my favorite Chicago coffee shop, watching happy people stroll in like they had not a care in the world. Meanwhile, I was the woman in the corner, worrying herself into a pretzel. We'd sacrificed everything to move our family from my husband's home state of Massachusetts to my home city of Chicago on a hunch from my heart, but I had no idea if it had all been a terrible mistake.

As I sat in the coffee shop, I was waiting to hear back on three major pieces of news—if our house in Massachusetts had gotten an offer, if I'd secured the university teaching job I'd just interviewed for, and if my memoir was going to be published. There were many worse hardships in the world—some I'd already been through, some I couldn't possibly fathom—but still, I was undone by the maddening uncertainty of it all. In addition to the what-ifs, I wondered how this move to Chicago would affect Geo—our toddler son—and Jamie—my nature-loving husband. The stress had already taken a toll. Would it destroy us?

As carefree patrons sipped coffee, I turned to my typical coping mechanism. I pulled out my journal and started scribbling. But what poured out of me that day was different than my usual ruminations. I don't know where it came from, and I'd never done it before, but I wrote a letter from my future-self to my present-self. I just needed someone to reassure me. And that "someone," apparently, was me.

As the sun streamed onto the pages, I wrote frantically, channeling her—my all-knowing, wiser voice. The words scrawled across the page, and sentences formed as if by their own volition. The ink dried on the paper, and I whispered the words to myself above the buzz of the espresso machine: *Take a breath, Sweetheart. Slow it down, Honey. It's all going to be OK.*

The reassurance washed over me, steadying my breath as I sipped my mocha and read the rest of the letter to myself. My inner-sage reassured me about the future—that it wouldn't always go as planned, but I would eventually live out my visions of teaching and publishing. The voice in her messages was so certain. I knew that she—whomever she was—was right. Throughout my life, I'd had deep knowings, a trust in myself, and an intuitive sense. I prided myself on being someone who followed her heart. Yet, like so many of us, I often didn't stop long enough to listen to its directions. I sought advice from therapists and friends, but I rarely asked myself what it was that I already knew. But that day was different. The words that poured out of me at the coffee shop changed me for good.

Looking back a decade later, I realize that my afternoon of letter writing was the beginning of something. It was the start of an important lesson—that life would almost always feel uncertain, and the future would continue to be an unknown. I'm writing this introduction at the end of 2022 from my home office in a Florida beach town as I look out at geckos scurrying up our live oak. Now that we've resided on the East Coast, the Midwest, and down South in homes, apartments, and an Airstream camper, I know that no town, house, or job will ever guarantee ease or joy. As the pandemic and other world traumas have proven, anything can happen. But I've learned that we can always consult and comfort ourselves. The ability to examine our intuition and calm our own fears is right here inside of us. We can always come back home to our own hearts.

So much has happened since that afternoon in the coffee shop: I did get the university teaching job, and an incredible female press published my memoir. Our sweet toddler has morphed into an inquisitive fourth grader who is reading a funny novel on the couch as I type. The fridge calendar shows my approaching 40th birthday, a milestone that has come with hard lessons and great gifts, like the fact that Jamie and I will soon celebrate 17 years together.

Of course, other things have happened, too. Letdowns. Roadblocks. COVID. The loss of loved ones. Many, many moves. I've pivoted and course-corrected, closing chapters on professions, places, and relationships that didn't quite fit anymore. I've opened doors on new chapters: launching a women's writing community, leading women's wellness retreats, and starting the *Heart of the Story* podcast.

But these days, I'm most proud of the things I'm reducing from my life: the overworking, the people-pleasing, the self-shaming. I no longer want to distract myself from my feelings or fill my life with the kind of noise that drowns out the whispers of my soul. I've learned that in order to follow our hearts, we must first give them room to speak. And my heart has told me that quality moments with my loved ones are much more important than any amount of productivity. It has told me that sitting in stillness is always a worthy endeavor. My heart has reminded me, over and over, that I can always return to it for guidance.

If your life has looked anything like mine, you've endured a million shocking transitions. Most things have not gone according to plan, and your lack of control has been maddening. You have faced overwhelming uncertainty again and again. Just when you think you've found your footing, the ground has crumbled beneath you. You have felt desperate for direction and reassurance, yet no one has given you the answers you desperately seek. Deep down, you know there's got to be another way, but your brain is so frazzled from all the trauma that it can barely focus. Rest assured. There is always another way, my love—the way of your heart. But how do you get there?

Over the last decade of my inner journey, I've compiled an array of story lessons and prompts for connecting straight to the source of our own wisdom. What follows is a collection of these little life moments that restored my spirit and taught me the grounding practices needed for the tumultuous times we continue to find ourselves in. Think of each chapter as a 15-minute retreat with a short story and some prompts for you to harness your inner sage. You can do them in order or let your heart choose at random. Since there are 28 chapters, you can complete one a day for four weeks, if you'd like. But there's no pressure. Trust that you'll know what you need.

I originally wrote these stories and letters as a sort of relief manual for myself when I forgot, once again, to sit, be still, listen, and trust myself. I didn't realize that my essays could appeal to other people until I read one aloud at a workshop, and a participant came up to me after. "That was exactly what I needed to hear right now," she said.

It occurred to me that I wasn't just writing to myself but to women everywhere, as a means of connection. I was writing to my sister—a social worker and my emotional confidant. I was writing to the other mamas who cherish their children and yearn for a minute alone. I was writing to women around the world, like those I've mentored as a writing coach, who've been through it all and have been brave enough to share their stories. What I say to my sister, to the other women, and now to you, dear reader, is the same thing my heart has whispered time and again:

Take a breath, Sweetheart.
Slow it down, Honey.
It's all going to be OK.
All you need is already here, right inside of you.

JOURNAL PROMPT: A LETTER FROM YOUR WISE HEART

I've been writing wise-voice letters to myself in my journal for years, and this is my go-to prompt every morning. It's also a fan favorite at my retreats. Here are the steps.

The Five Cs: Ceremony, Compassion, Connection, Clearing, and Clarity.

CEREMONY

Create a simple ceremony. Sitting down with your favorite mug or journal can make this exercise feel sacred. Write by the glow of a candle. Get cozy in a nest of blankets. Make an altar of cherished objects that you add to each day. Do whatever brings you joy.

COMPASSION

Set a timer. Perfectionism is the enemy of self-compassion, so set a timer for 10 minutes and tell yourself to just write whatever comes, no matter how imperfect.

Channel your wiser-self. Visualize the you that is months or years in the future, the part of your heart that has emerged from your current hardship. What wisdom does it carry?

Start with a compassionate greeting. Address yourself from the perspective of this wiser-self. Speak the way you would to a beloved. *Hi, darling. Good morning, my love.*

CONNECTION

Acknowledge your feelings. What is your wiser-self observing without judgment? State what they notice. *I can see that you're hurting. This is a tough decision, isn't it?*

Access your fears and desires. What is your greatest worry? Your strongest longing?

State what your heart knows. What does perspective offer to the situation? Be the scribe as you channel your innate wisdom. Try these prompts: *I know that you're scared, but I also know… Your heart knows that… Your deepest knowing is…*

CLEARING

List what you can let go of. Dump your obsessive thoughts onto the page, as well as anything you can't control. What's not serving you anymore?

List what you're grateful for and proud of. Nothing clears negativity like gratitude.

CLARITY

Request the next right step. Listen for the answer. It might take the form of advice, a mantra, or a nudge. The solution is not always a big gesture: *Rest. Pause. Stay. Hug.*

Close with love and read what you wrote. Be amazed by the wisdom that came simply because you asked and made the time to listen.

LETTER EXAMPLE

Good morning Sweetheart,

You've been through it, haven't you? My goodness, have you suffered. Your heart has been shattered. Weep for it. Go ahead. Let those tears roll. Lay down the weight of all you've carried, the illusion of control you've been gripping onto so tightly. Because today, the sun is shining, and the birds are chirping. Today, you rubbed the warm bellies of your puppies. Your husband made you laugh as he played the air flute. Today, you held your cuddly son in your arms while he rubbed his eyes awake. He's almost as tall as you, but you can still lift him into your arms, and for that, you are grateful. But even as you hugged him, terror flooded your brain. You're always so afraid that the other shoe will drop. You long to experience joy without feeling the fear that it will be taken away. But you know, deep down, that your gratitude doesn't erase the hardship of your past. Your hard past does not rule out your current gratitude. The two coexist. They always have and always will. Because you've known deep hardship, feel free to revel in this bliss. Don't feel ashamed of your good fortune, Honey. Feel it; absorb it with your entire being. These moments of joy are the jewels you live for. Wear them, like crystals, around your soul.

I am here, holding you. Always.

Love,
Your Wise Heart

Your Turn: Light a candle or sit in your favorite spot. If you're having trouble settling, set a timer for 10 minutes.

If mental clutter arises, like tasks from your to-do list, draw a box in the margins to dump any intruding thoughts and return to letter writing.

Date _____

Dear _____, (Write a compassionate greeting.)

I see that you're dealing with this right now:

_____

_____

_____

_____

_____

It's hard/frustrating/overwhelming to:

_____

_____

_____

_____

Your heart's greatest longing is:

_____

_____

Your heart's deepest knowing is:

You can let go of these things that aren't serving you anymore:

I'm so proud of you for:

_____

_____

_____

_____

Your next right step is:

_____

_____

_____

_____

_____

Here for you always,
Your Wise Heart

CHAPTER 2

Somebody, Someday

My professional writing career began with me almost flunking out of college. I'd been a stellar student all my life, but when I entered the University of Illinois as a nutrition major, chemistry got the best of me. Each time I sat in that 200-person lecture hall amongst the cornfields of Champaign-Urbana, it felt like the professor was speaking a different language. So, rather than asking for help, I just stopped going to class. But unbeknownst to me, report cards were being mailed back home.

The envelope arrived when I was at my parents' house over Christmas break.

I was all dressed up, heading out to a party with my hometown friends. As I put on my winter coat, my mom opened my report card—a 1.8 GPA. Academic probation.

In a minute, she was levitating over me, growling, "You'd better get your act together, or you're moving back home, getting a job, and paying your own way through college." I was the first person in my entire family to attend a four-year university, and my hardworking parents were making great sacrifices to send me there. My mom was not about to let me party my way out of a once-in-a-lifetime opportunity.

So, I returned to Champaign and studied the only thing I liked: literature. As an English major, my mind clicked again. My grades soared. I was still partying, though, and at a bar one night, another aspiring writer told me about a magazine where I could submit my writing.

The next day, I sat down and wrote my first short story and submitted it. To my great surprise, it got accepted for publication.

Could I actually do this? Be a writer? It suddenly seemed like a very faint possibility. Then, for my 19th birthday, my roommate Jenny gave me a life-changing gift: an anthology of *The Best American Short Stories*. Inside, she'd penciled my name into the table of contents with a dot-dot-dot after it, as if I were one of the writers. Or that I could be one day.

Two years later, I applied to 10 MFA programs. I got rejected from all but two and was waitlisted by both. After graduation, all my friends were getting well-paying jobs, but I moved back home and worked as a waitress while I waited to hear back from the grad schools.

I thought maybe Jenny was wrong. I couldn't become a writer. No program wanted me. I couldn't get a steady job. I volunteered at the local newspaper, and they put me on the police blotter beat. It was awful. But then they let me write a couple of articles, and the few people who read them said they were decent. Maybe this writing thing was possible after all.

I'd walk around Chicago on the weekends, look at the big newspaper buildings, and dream of working at one. I refused to let my current state be my fate. So, every week that summer, I called Columbia College Chicago, one of the waitlist grad schools, until they were so worn out by me that they announced my acceptance. And after my mom's urging, I applied for an internship at *Chicago* magazine.

Suddenly there I was, walking up Michigan Avenue to the Tribune Tower every day, living my dream of working at a fancy magazine office, then walking south to Columbia every night and penning my stories. It didn't matter that I was scraping by and living in a tiny studio apartment. After two glorious years, I'd written a book and gotten a diploma.

And then, I moved cross country to Massachusetts to be with my now-husband. I had no writing community, no book contract, and was making minimum wage as an adjunct professor. My belief in myself was fading. Just when I needed a boost of confidence, Jenny—my dear old college roommate—mailed me a chapter from Maya Angelou's book *Mom & Me & Mom*. I opened up the envelope, took out the photocopied pages, and sat down in my living room to read them. It was late at night, and I felt restless like I was destined for something bigger, but life was not giving me any breaks.

I carefully read the chapter, which was about Maya as a young woman trying to make it in the world. One day, when she was 22, her mother invited her over for red rice. After the meal, Maya and her mother were walking down the street in San Francisco when her mother turned to her and said, "Baby, I've been thinking, and now I am sure. You are the greatest woman I've ever met." She said that Maya belonged in the same category as Dr. Mary McCleod Bethune and Eleanor Roosevelt.

Maya asked herself, "What if she's right?...Suppose I really am going to become somebody. Imagine." Maya said that at that moment, she decided to stop some of her bad habits. And she ends the story with this: "Imagine. I might really become somebody. Someday."

She was 22. She had no idea that she'd become a dancer, a writer, a civil rights activist, that she'd publish seven autobiographies, three books of essays, several books of poetry, plays, movies, and television shows, and that she'd become the inaugural poet in 1993.

She was simply 22 and had the thought, *What if I could become somebody, someday?*

I wept because I yearned for someone to say to me, "You're the greatest woman I've ever met," but by Jenny sending me those pages, it felt like someone out there believed in me. And what if I believed in myself? What if I might become somebody, someday? [1]

I decided to stop my own bad habits of playing it small, of just trying to be grateful

---

[1] Angelou, *Mom & Me & Mom*

for the minuscule opportunities given to women. I decided to take matters into my own hands. If publishers and university hiring committees were not knocking on my door, I would knock on theirs. So I sent my memoir proposal to publishers. I applied for full-time university teaching jobs. I asked around even when they weren't actively hiring. I started coaching other women on how to develop and publish their stories. I did it all not by waiting to get permission but by giving myself permission. I kept believing in the possibility that I might become somebody. Someday.

When I got hired full time by a university, when I walked into a bookstore and saw my own memoir on its shelves, when my female authors thanked me in the acknowledgment sections of their published books, I thought back to that anthology Jenny had given me at 19, about the seed of belief she had planted in my brain.

And now, I want to plant that very seed in your brain.

If you think that no one in the entire universe believes in you, imagine you are getting this story in the mail. And when you read this, you will know deep in your soul that you are going to be somebody someday. That you are somebody. Right now.

JOURNALING PROMPTS

Address Your Wounds

What are your unrealized dreams? Why do they call to you? If you accomplished them, how would you feel?

What self-critical thoughts are standing in the way of your self-belief?

What are the external obstacles to your dreams that seem overwhelming?

Channel Your Wisdom

If there was nothing standing in the way of your dreams, what would you do?

What bad habits would you let go of? Do less of?

What new good habits would you implement? What steps would you start taking?

What is the thing you're yearning to read, see, etc.? (This is the very thing you're being called to create.)

What permission can you give yourself that you've been waiting for someone else to give you?

Letter: Write about the moments when you've overcome obstacles so you can connect the dots in hindsight and garner lessons from your journey.

Date _____

Dear _____ ,

I know that you want to accomplish _____ but you have false beliefs like:

_____

_____

_____

_____

_____

_____

_____

_____

which are standing in the way of your self-belief.

Please remember, Sweetheart, that you've overcome so many obstacles before, like:

_____

_____

_____

And it all led to you achieving:

Here are the lessons you learned from those experiences:

Someday you are going to become:

And you are somebody right now because:

Never forget that.

Love,
Your Tenacious Heart

P.S. Don't forget to read this back to yourself.

CHAPTER 3

Put the Paintbrush Down

Just after Jamie and I got married, we signed up for a couples' painting class in Newton, Massachusetts. Neither of us was Picasso. We just wanted to drink a little wine and harness our silly side. I longed to remember the carefree person I'd been before the mortgage and the professional pressure and the having-a-baby discussions.

The night of the workshop, I changed out of my buttoned-up professor attire and into a flowy skirt I hadn't worn since our dating years. When I came down the stairs, Jamie whistled.

"Well, hello," he said with a grin. He held out his hand, escorting me to our car. During the whole drive to the city, a long-forgotten energy flowed through me. Freedom. Ease. Excitement.

We shuffled through the snowy parking lot, giddily entering the warm studio with the other couples, and I got our seats while Jamie went up to the bar. The workshop description had explained that we'd jointly paint one winter landscape, but there were two easels at our station. I wondered how we would make our styles match if we were each painting separate canvases. Before I could think too much about it, Jamie returned, handing me a glass of red.

"Cheers, Love," I said, and we clinked our glasses. Jamie whispered something silly in my ear, and it felt like the early stages of flirting. I giggled. This was going to be fun.

The teacher stood on an elevated platform and began her instruction.

"Each partner should choose an element of the landscape, like the trees or river, and paint across both canvases," she said, demonstrating with her paintbrush. This would unite the painting, despite having two different artists.

So, Jamie painted the sky across the canvases while I painted the mountains. With each swooping stroke, we were bonding, enjoying ourselves. Like the other couples, we were laughing and nudging each other. But as the teacher gave more instructions, I noticed that I was a bit more "detail-oriented," going back to refine, whereas Jamie followed each step, seemed satisfied enough, and put his brush down. I resisted the urge to touch up his work.

Then one of us had to paint the cardinal on the tree branch. I volunteered.

In order to create the tiny beak, I needed a finer brush. I rifled through the mason jar, finding no skinny ones. So I did my best, dabbing intently, but the beak seemed too big.

I stepped back to get a better perspective.

There was no doubt about it. The beak was almost bigger than the bird's head.

Jamie said something, but I wasn't listening. My obsessive brain wanted the beak just right, and I wouldn't stop until it was.

I hunched over the canvas, stabbing it with tiny strokes. Since the beak was too big, I had to make the body proportional. I started to repaint the chest and wings.

My compulsive focus felt all-consuming, as it had for most of my upbringing. My mom, stepdad, and biological father were extremely hardworking individuals. Any job done was a job done well, even when it came to tedious tasks, like when Mom would spend hours straightening my part and curling my pigtails. I'd inherited this eye for detail, but something went awry when I translated it into perfectionism. In my writing and professional realms, you'd better believe that I would do my very, very, very, very best, but this didn't bode well when it came to casual date nights with my husband.

I stepped back. The bird had taken over the branch—like a pterodactyl on a twig.

"Now the body's too big," I complained to Jamie.

"It's fine," he said.

I shook my head in disagreement. The other couples were laughing louder, but our station was eerily silent.

Right then, the instructor announced that it was time for a gallery walk, signaling us to amble around and look at the other artists' finished products. Chairs screeched as everyone got up. Couples sipped their wine and moved clockwise around the room in pairs, complimenting other people's canvases. Except for me. I was tempted to start "fixing" the trees to make them proportional to the bird.

"Nader," Jamie said, sensing my inner struggle. "Put the paintbrush down."

That was impossible. The perfectionist in me raged. *But it's not acceptable. It's not done.* I would not be satisfied until it was fixed.

Then I saw the couple next to us hugging each other and smiling. I looked over at Jamie, who was sitting quietly, staring at the floor.

What am I doing? I thought.

In my pursuit of perfectionism, I'd missed the entire point.

If I touched up the bird anymore, I would ruin the whole thing. If I hadn't perfected it in the first place, our work would have looked better than it did now. And in the bigger picture of life, maybe it wasn't just the mortgage and work pressures that had robbed my carefree nature. Maybe it was my very own perfectionism.

I slowly put the paintbrush down, then I reached over and squeezed Jamie's hand.

"Let's go look at the other paintings," I said.

* * *

Jamie has proudly hung our canvases in every place we've lived, and I've gotten used to seeing our mediocre painting on display. Yes, my cardinal looks like a toucan, but a beautiful thing came out of the experience. When I am "fixing" things, Jamie will catch me out of the corner of his eye and say, "Put the paintbrush down."

It's our bat signal. It means: Nothing is that serious. You're missing the point of the experience. Your mental control is actually destroying the moment.

It means: Stop what you are doing. Put down whatever is in your hands. Step back. Notice the beauty of your creations. Embrace your ordinariness. Nurture your flaws. Then hang them on your walls for all to see.

JOURNALING PROMPTS

Address Your Wounds

In what areas of your life do you need to "put the paintbrush down"?

Where have you lost your carefree nature?

Channel Your Wisdom

What aspects of your "flawed" self do you enjoy?

What hobbies, activities, people, places, make you feel most carefree?

Can you practice imperfection? What experiences can you partake in where the goal is to be messy and imperfect and vulnerable and lighthearted?

A Little Fun: Draw a picture of yourself in your most carefree, fun-loving state. Where are you? What are you wearing? What are you doing? Who are you with? (Don't expect yourself to be Picasso. Stick figures are welcome.)

Letter: Write a love letter from your Proud Heart to your inner perfectionist.

Date _____

Dear _____,

I see that you're trying to "fix" and control these things:

_____
_____
_____
_____

But it's actually making things worse in the following ways:

_____
_____
_____
_____

You can put the paintbrush down by:

_____
_____
_____
_____

Remember, your imperfections are your superpowers. These quirks are what others love most about you:

_____

_____

_____

_____

I'm proudest of you in the moments when you are your non-striving self, like when you:

_____

_____

_____

_____

Cheers,
Your Proud Heart

P.S. Don't forget to read this back to yourself.

CHAPTER 4
Loosen the Edges

When Geo was a toddler, he wanted things that didn't make sense to us, like milk mixed with juice. Every night, he'd stand before the open refrigerator in his Thomas the Train pajamas, and when I'd pull out the 2% to make his bottle, he'd say, "I want juice too, Mama."

I tried to explain curdling and tummy aches, but he insisted on this weird concoction. He wanted what he wanted when he wanted it. And when he didn't get it, he flailed his limbs. We tried to prevent his toddler rebellion with structure and routine, which worked. Sometimes.

One afternoon, I took Geo for a walk around Ravenswood, our northern Chicago neighborhood. I pushed Geo's stroller down Damen, under the screeching L train, and we arrived at Welles Park. A Little League team played on the corner diamond, and I noticed a distinct smell mixing with the dust from the baseball field—a light, doughy, vanilla scent.

"What's that, Mama?" Geo asked, leaning forward in his stroller and pointing at the Crepes in the Park stand. Inside, two cooks hovered over a circular hot plate. The older cook poured the batter, and as we got closer, the scent of the crepe was irresistible.

"I want that," Geo said, trying to climb out of his stroller. I knew I should stick to our routine and say, "No snacks. It's almost dinner." But in that moment, I saw something of myself in him, some impulsive instinct that desires the unknown and seeks it out.

"Let's just see what they have," I said, which is exactly the same thing I'd said to myself when I was 24 and entering a crepe shop in Lincoln Park for the first time.

* * *

It was 2007. I had just received the news that Jamie had been offered a new job, not in Chicago, as had been the plan, but in Massachusetts, and we'd have to continue our 800-mile-apart courtship. My parents said I should keep living with them and save money while I finished out my last year of grad school. But I knew it might be the only time in my life I had the opportunity to live alone, so I looked for apartments in the city. When I saw that studio, I simply thought, *I want that. Now.* Because even though the apartment had a kitchen the size of a shoe box and walls with water damage, it also had a window facing east. The building in the next lot had just been torn down, so outside my window was the shrine of St. Francis, North Pond, and Lake Michigan. Lake-freaking-Michigan, right outside my window.

I moved in at the end of the summer, on the cusp of my 24th birthday. As soon as I set up my day bed and my kitchen table in that little room, I did whatever I wanted whenever I wanted. It wasn't premeditated; I just asked myself, *What do you really want to do right now?* And then I tried to do just that. Mostly I wanted to walk around and explore the city. I would take the red line home from grad school, get off at Fullerton, peek inside all the brownstone windows, then take a left on Clark and a right on St. James, which was exactly what I was doing the September afternoon that I stopped in front of the Algerian creperie, Icosium Kafé.

I'd smelled that doughy vanilla scent during my previous walks home from the red line, but I was on a tight budget. I knew I should be using my cash on nourishing meals, but ever since I'd moved into my studio, I'd been perpetually hungry, which was how I always felt when I was in love with life. I wanted to try everything.

The sign said "Crepe and Coffee Palace," and it sold sweet and savory crepes. When scanning the menu, my eyes automatically looked for grilled chicken, so trained were they to find the "right" option. In fact, it felt like I was always scanning menus and situations to look for what I *should* choose, not what I *wanted* to choose. Usually, something lavish, like a decadent dessert, was saved for celebrating special occasions with a group. But at the crepe café, I wondered why I still felt I needed permission to want something. Could I not grant my own wish? And did it always have to be thought-out or rational? I saw a large jar of Nutella behind the counter, and I asked myself, *What do you really want to eat?* My mind chanted, *Chocolate, chocolate, chocolate.*

The wiry old chef poured batter onto a hot plate and spread it with a mini rake. Then, in a matter of seconds, his thin spatula lifted the edges and flipped it. Watching his artful lifting and flipping made something in me shift too. I considered that maybe all the "shoulds" I'd learned weren't the end-all-be-all. Maybe *my* desires were worthy of paying attention to.

The chef smoothed the crepe out on the counter and smeared a glob of rich Nutella into the center, which instantly softened and spread. Then he folded the crepe, drizzled zigzags of caramel, and used a sifter to sprinkle powdered sugar over it. Finally, he scooped a dollop of whipped cream onto the top and sent it home with me in a styrofoam box. Throughout the two-block walk up Clark, the smells of hazelnut and caramel teased me, prevailing over bus exhaust. When I entered my apartment, I locked the door and opened my curtains to reveal that beautiful lake. Then I sat at my tiny kitchen table, and I ate dessert alone for the very first time.

I could still hear September on the other side of my thin window—a mixture of taxi honks and lake wind—but, for the most part, it was sunny and very still in my little studio. I sat at my table and cut the crepe into petite pieces. The Nutella oozed out, and the powdered sugar dissolved into the pools of chocolate. The scent of crepe dough permeated my apartment. I forked a piece into my mouth and let it sit on my tongue until it melted over my taste buds. It was both light and dense at the same time. I chewed more slowly than I ever had, feeling so incredibly in love in that moment—with life, with the city, with myself. Delighting in my own company, I was honoring the sacred ceremony of relishing every bite without regret.

In 20 minutes, the crepe was gone, and in May, I was gone too, driving to Massachusetts with my diploma and other possessions in the trunk of my Cavalier. Flash forward six more years, and I was back in Illinois with Jamie and baby Geo in tow. When we drove through Lincoln Park, I was shocked to find Icosium Kafé replaced by a modern salon and my lake view blocked by a tower of million-dollar condos.

What had brought me back, besides being homesick for my family, was that same feeling that I had experienced when I was 24—a personal desire I needed to honor. The last year we'd lived in Massachusetts, I'd heard the non-conforming whispers of my soul—*I know I should want this: the charming old house and the rural ease, but I don't. I want the city, my writing career, and my Chicago community.* So, I'd chosen the Nutella over the chicken, and we'd made the impractical leap to move cross country to the city with a toddler.

* * *

Back at the Crepes in the Park stand, Geo watched the batter spread across the hot plate. The older cook told the younger cook, "So, you wait a couple of seconds for the batter to harden." He grabbed his spatula. "Then, what you do is, you loosen the edges, and you flip quickly."

Geo held the foil-wrapped plate the whole way home to our apartment, smelling it and grinning with the same anticipation I'd had while walking up Clark to my studio all those years ago. As I pushed his stroller, I tried to put my finger on the exact emotion fueled by that light, doughy vanilla scent when I was 24 and living in Chicago.

It wasn't exactly that I had loved the city. I'd loved what living alone in the city had allowed me to do: listen to my gut impulses and deem myself worthy of honoring them.

It had loosened my edges. It had flipped them quickly.

JOURNALING PROMPTS

Address Your Wounds

What are the "shoulds" you've heard your whole life?

What are the "shoulds" you're hearing the most right now?

What are the "shoulds" that are no longer serving you?

What is holding you back from rejecting the "shoulds"? Whose judgment or disappointment are you most afraid of?

Channel Your Wisdom

What do you desire right now? (Don't think, just answer. ☺)

What do you want to do this week, month, year? Today?

What is something you're yearning to try?

To wear?

To see?

To touch?

To hear?

To smell?

To eat?

Letter: Write yourself a letter from your Worthy Heart.

Date _____

Dear _____ ,

Here are the things you deeply desire even if they don't seem practical:

_____
_____
_____
_____
_____
_____

But some of the unworthy messages you're hearing are:

_____
_____
_____
_____
_____
_____

What would happen if you believed that you were worthy of these pleasures?

_____
_____
_____
_____

So, here are some things you are going to do and savor today:

Pleasure is your birthright,
Your Worthy Heart

P.S. Don't forget to read this back to yourself.

CHAPTER 5

Pay It Forward

We'd been living in Chicago for a couple of years when my memoir was about to go to print. My publishing house was hosting a retreat in Arizona, and it sounded amazing. A bunch of the women writers would get to meet each other and swap notes. There would be a professional photographer there to take our author headshots, a video crew to record our book trailers, and a host of great speakers to walk us through promoting our books. It would be beyond beneficial. But since I would be traveling a lot in the spring for my book tour, there wasn't extra money in our budget for this retreat.

And then, a woman—a total stranger who'd bought a ticket—could no longer make it. So she gave the ticket to me. Free of charge. All she asked was that I pay it forward to another woman in need when I could. And she wasn't doing this for recognition. She asked to remain anonymous if I shared the news with others that I'd been gifted the retreat ticket.

To say I was shocked is an understatement. I did not know this woman. But I knew women like her. She reminded me of my friend Cheryl, who had swept in at the most needed time in Massachusetts to pamper me.

* * *

Geo was about 10 months old when we put our Massachusetts house on the market to move to Chicago. Every other day, in addition to raising an infant, teaching, and creating online curricula, I'd have to ready our house for a showing. This wasn't so easy to do when our entire first level was a baby gymnasium. There was a pack-and-play with a changing table permanently fixed in our living room. There were all sorts of machines—a swing, a walker, a bouncy seat. There were board books and rattles and stuffed animals. There were building blocks and toy cars and boppies and teething rings. Our cute house no longer looked cute. It looked like a baby had vomited everywhere because, well, it had.

Oh, and we had mice. Well, a mouse. Like many old New England homes that shelter critters during the winter, ours had become home to a certain rodent who would traipse around inside our walls at night. I couldn't even think about the germs the mouse was spreading on the same furniture Geo touched and chewed on daily. And prospective buyers might not be too keen on rodents either. One night, Jamie was watching TV in his recliner when he saw the mouse bravely scurry across our living room floor and head for the kitchen. He looked everywhere but couldn't find it.

On a Friday night after the house had been on the market for months, we decided to treat ourselves to a family dinner out, a rarity. We had a showing the next day, and we'd spent the better part of our afternoon tidying up the house. When we came home from dinner and entered our kitchen, we heard a strange noise. As I set Geo's car seat carrier on the floor and took off my coat, animal squeaks emanated from the oven, and I realized that the mouse had found its way inside the back but couldn't find its way out. It was trapped somewhere within the deeper inner workings of the wiring. I couldn't. Even. Deal. It was all just too much.

We had raised a newborn baby on our own; we'd purged our house and put it on the market; we'd job hunted; we'd planned a cross-country move from Jamie's home state in Massachusetts to mine in Illinois. We'd done seemingly insurmountable things. But I could not, for the life of me, even contemplate how to find this poor mouse and free it from the oven before prospective buyers came over the next day for a showing.

Surely, they'd walk in with their realtor only to hear mouse squeals and turn right back around. We'd never sell our house, and we'd never move to Chicago, and we'd never have family nearby to help with Geo, and we'd never have a date or an uninterrupted night's sleep, and I'd never look young and rested ever again in my entire life. Ever. (Like most people's catastrophizing, mine always ended in "never" or "ever.")

Maybe the universe had a way of communicating that I was in over my head and deeply needed some R and R, but the next day, my dear friend Cheryl said she was taking me for a rejuvenating overnight at a resort spa concert venue. This was not my normal life. I had never, up until that point, been to a spa. I'd only ever gotten my nails done three times—junior prom, senior prom, and my wedding.

Cheryl and her husband were originally Jamie's friends, but Cheryl and I had become closer since my pregnancy. She was always so big-hearted—offering to take pregnancy portraits at a nearby park when I was near my due date, and after Geo was born, coming over to rock him so I could shower and eat. Cheryl and Billy had some perks at the resort, and for whatever generous reason, Cheryl chose to use them on me.

While Jamie was disconnecting the gas line and pulling our oven away from the wall, then dismantling the back of it until he found the mouse, I was packing a bag with clothes and makeup that I had not worn since before pregnancy. I was going to wear a clean dress (gasp!) and go to a concert (double gasp!) and sleep all night in a hotel room, with no midnight feedings (unimaginable!).

The second I picked Cheryl up, I felt free from all of my anxiety, not having to worry about a car seat and diaper bag. Cheryl and I talked and laughed the whole drive. When we arrived, we went up to our nice hotel room and unpacked our bags. Then it was time for the spa. We changed into swimsuits and fluffy robes and entered the lounge with its relaxing music and cucumber water. We talked to the other female spa goers, and I thought I would faint from happiness. I got a pedicure, then we got dressed up, and the icing on the cake—Cheryl curled my hair, and we got into the elevator to head to the arena.

My heart felt full as we sang along with the concert crowd. I realized the true gift Cheryl had given me. In each situation, there was nothing in it for her. There was no ulterior motive. She saw a woman who needed help, and she gave it.

* * *

Flash forward a few years later, and I experienced a similar form of generosity from the woman who gifted me the ticket to the Arizona retreat. I was so used to self-sufficiency that I almost didn't know how to accept the offering, but I felt so fortunate.

The retreat weekend was beyond my expectations. I left winter behind and headed to sunny Sedona. My days consisted of jogs among the boulders and talks with talented women. Afterward, I sent my gifter a thank you note and a journal, but she was happiest to learn that I was planning to pay it forward by giving a scholarship to a student at a retreat I was leading that winter and another spot in an online class I was teaching.

I emailed two women writer friends who most needed generosity at that time, offering them the retreat and class opportunities. Their reactions were the best gifts. They were as grateful and as shocked as I was when I'd received such generosity, but it was even more fulfilling being on the giving end.

And when they asked me how they could repay me, I simply said, "Pay it forward."

JOURNALING PROMPTS

Address Your Wounds

In what areas of your life do you feel a gaping wound or void?

What self-care are you desperate for? (Sleep? Time alone? A meal cooked by someone else?)

Who might be willing to help you? What's standing in the way of receiving their abundance?

Channel Your Wisdom

What have you already been given?

What do you have plenty of (tangible and intangible)?

What can you possibly give to others? Who can you give it to?

Letter: Abundance is in the giving and the receiving. Choose someone you'd like to thank or someone you'd like to offer generosity to. Write a note to them. You can choose whether or not to actually send it.

Date _____

Dear _____ ,

Sincerely,

_____

CHAPTER 6

Again

I was in San Miguel, Mexico, presenting at a writing workshop, when I walked down the crowded, cobblestone street toward the hotel conference center and something caught my eye.

It was a mother carrying her child—not in a sling or stroller, but in her very own arms. Behind her, another mother carried her toddler. These women traversed the steep street, and I waited for them to shift or struggle, but they toted those children like extensions of themselves.

As the rest of San Miguel streamed past me, I stood in the middle of the sidewalk, wondering what was halting me. Maybe it was jealousy—that familiar envy I'd known as Jamie and I had tried, unsuccessfully, to have a child. During those years, I'd injected hormone shots and wailed over failed IVF cycles while every other woman in the world seemed to sport a baby bump.

But as I watched the mothers, I knew that this feeling was different. After all, Jamie and I had finally conceived Geo, and he was a happy, healthy three-year-old.

I realized that, back home, I had never seen a mother navigate the neighborhood with a newborn in her arms. Sure, I'd seen plenty of infants being transported in all-terrain strollers and baby backpacks, but usually, when women carried their swaddled children in their arms, it was at home while nursing and rocking them. The intimacy was behind closed doors. But in San Miguel, it was on full display in a way that made my heart ache.

During Geo's infancy, I'd carried him around our Massachusetts home like a football, his belly resting on my forearm. In that position, he didn't cry. In that position, he fell asleep, content. He was always attached to me—nursing from me, rocking in my lap. At night, I sat in the glider under the skylight in his tiny nursery, and I sang "You Are My Sunshine" over and over again until his eyes grew heavy.

As the months passed, other things grew heavy, too, like my mood, weighed down by the overwhelm and loneliness of raising a newborn without family nearby. As a means of efficiency, I bought a Baby Bjorn so I could be hands-free and do dishes while bouncing Geo to sleep.

Then, just after his first birthday, we moved to Chicago. Geo learned to walk, but it took him an eternity to descend the stairs of our third-floor apartment in Ravenswood. So, to save time, I carried him.

Every morning, as we were rush, rush, rushing, I struggled down the steps with my work bag on one arm and Geo in the other. Usually, I'd strain to keep him on my hip, and I'd say, "You're heavy, buddy." I said it so much that one day when we approached the landing, Geo said, "Heavy."

I stopped in the middle of the stairwell. His tone had reflected the same frustration I used when I said, "You're heavy," as if he were a burden, something unwieldy to carry. The stairs were a burden, and the pace of life was a burden. But he, my beautiful son, was not a burden. I never wanted him to think that.

I stopped saying "heavy" when I carried him.

Geo learned to say other things, including song requests. "Bus" meant that I should sing "Wheels on the Bus" and "sun-shy" meant that I should sing "You Are My Sunshine." For a couple of months, when I finished a song, Geo would clap his hands and say, "Again," but then he started cutting me off mid-chorus and asking for another tune. Eventually, when I headed to his glider for nighttime cuddles and lullabies, he said, "Bed," and pointed to his crib. This cut our nighttime routine by 30 minutes, allowing me a half hour to myself—an extravagance that hadn't existed since his birth, and some nights, I relished in the ease—the luxury of checking emails or watching TV.

But, then, there I was, on my own at a writer's conference in San Miguel, seeing mothers carrying their children everywhere, and I was desperate to embrace Geo, to hold onto this little boy stage where he still desired my affection. Maybe the women carried their children because the stone streets weren't stroller-friendly. There was also the very complicated fact of privilege—that so many women don't have access to a sturdy stroller, to equal-paying jobs, to child care. But this moment opened my eyes to the very gift awaiting me at home: carrying a child who would, too soon, be able to sprint up and down the hills on his own.

* * *

Back in Chicago after the trip, when it was time for Geo to go to bed, I carried him into his room, and when he pointed to his crib, I said, "Let's sit for a while." We sunk into the glider, and I cradled him. I relished in it, stamped it in my mind—his head nuzzled into my neck, his fuzzy hair under my chin, his sweet soapy smell. His body was double the length of my arm, and he was over 30 pounds, but still, in that moment, he felt light.

I sang him "sun-shy." And maybe he could feel my lightness, too, because he let me sing the whole song.

And when I was done, he said, "Again."

JOURNALING PROMPTS

Address Your Wounds

What are the ways you find yourself looking at others with jealousy?

What do they have (emotionally) that you are yearning for?

Channel Your Wisdom

What are the things that took effort and caused exhaustion in the past but that you look back on now and treasure?

Why do these memories mean so much to you?

Letter: Write a time capsule letter to yourself, reminding you of what to cherish in the now.

Date _____

Hi Sweetheart,

I'm 10 years down the road, realizing all the gifts you have before you right this very second. By noticing them now, you honor them. They are:

_____

_____

_____

_____

_____

_____

_____

_____

_____

_____

_____

_____

_____

_____

_____

_____

_____

_____

_____

_____

_____

_____

_____

_____

_____

Hold them in your arms, my love,
Your Future Heart

P.S. Don't forget to read this back to yourself.

CHAPTER 7

Remember Today

Sometimes when I'm in a dark place, I need a reminder that things will be OK again in the not-too-distant future. So, when Geo was a toddler, I started documenting the good times, and I compiled them into a "Remember Letter" that I could read for some uplifting support during a hard time. Here's what I wrote:

Dear Stressed-out Self,

Next year, when it's April in Chicago, and you are still wearing your winter coat, remember today.

Even though it seems that the grey clouds will never part, that the tree buds will never bloom, and that you'll never get out of this mucky rut of negativity, you will. You will wake up to a morning like today, where the sun shines so strongly that your bedroom is bright even through the blinds. The robins chirp in the oak tree, and the bunnies scamper through the grass. You leave home in a flowy skirt as bright as the new tulips along the hedges. People ride their bikes to work and power-walk to the beach. And the sun shines on all of it.

When Geo is shouting and stomping because you mixed his yogurt with a spoon and he wanted it "flat" (whatever that means), remember today.

He's freshly bathed and in a onesie, smelling minty as he sits in your lap for storytime. His soft hair tickles your chin. The sun is setting, and the living room glows pink as you both snuggle into the worn leather chair by the window. You're reading one of his favorite books, Froggy Goes to Hawaii. *Froggy is clumsy and forgetful, and every time Froggy slips or says something silly, Geo lets out a contagious giggle, and soon, you're both vibrating with laughter.*

When you and Jamie are annoyed with each other, remember today.

He's watching you play baseball with Geo, giving you that look—the smitten smile of wonderment like you are the most incredible woman he's ever met. You've been together for a third of your life, and still, you look at each other with awe. Later, he cooks dinner and serves you before himself. He always does, always has. In bed, he stops watching his tablet and closes your book. He sweeps the hair from your eyes and says, "I love you, wifey"—not because of anything you've done, just because of who you are.

Remember today when you're tired and want to sleep in.

Your alarm goes off for 6 a.m. yoga class, and you leave the studio an hour later, skipping on air, energized and relaxed, stretched and sore. The endorphins are pumping through you, putting you in a mood that no one can damper. On the way home, you stop at a coffee shop to get a mocha for yourself and an iced latte for Jamie. You hold the door open for other customers just because it's a nice thing to do. Back home, you make a smoothie for Geo and present your boys with their treats. Jamie is buttoning his shirt while singing to the radio, and Geo is driving a toy car along the floor. You're so grateful for them that you want to hug the universe. Instead, you hand them their drinks, and the three of you stand around, sipping on sweetness.

Remember today when you feel lonely because your extended family is so small.

Mom spends an hour in highway traffic to help you get ready for Geo's birthday and arrives armed with chips and dip, fruit salad, and a veggie tray. She hangs streamers. She fills a bucket with water and cleaner, then gets down on her hands and knees to scrub the floor. Your bathroom floor. You think of all the other people in the world who would voluntarily clean the grout around your toilet, and the only other person on that list is your sister, which says a lot because she hates cleaning. Besides Jamie, Mom and Dana are the only ones on the planet who would do anything for you. They'd walk, fly, and run any distance to take care of you if you needed it. As Mom scours the old tiles and Dana calls to say she picked up the birthday cake, you think, "That, right there, that's love."

When you've overbooked yourself yet again, remember today.

It's a lazy Saturday. You, Jamie, and Geo wear comfy clothes all afternoon and lounge on the couch, cuddling and playing. Then, when Geo naps, you read a good book in bed and doze off too. At night, you order Thai takeout and the three of you eat rice that inevitably gets everywhere. "How did you get rice in your belly button?" you ask Geo during bath time, and he just laughs. This little reprieve is so rejuvenating that you wake up the next day ready to take on the world.

Remember today when you realize your friendships have faded over the years.

You're at a rosé tasting in Lakeview with your college friends. The group is taking a break from discussing parenting woes and the state of the world. Instead, you're all in the present and giggling over silly things like you did when you were 18 and eating pizza on your dorm room floor.

Remember today when you've received a rejection on an essay you love.

You've just won an award for your book, and you're telling your true, emotional stories to a crowd of women who are nodding along with you because that's what it's all about, isn't it? This writing thing? Isn't the whole point of every story to tell each other, "You are not alone"? To not only say, "See me," but also, "I see you."

Above all else, the most important thing to remember is this: In order to store today in your memory, you have to live it. Fully. Not while distracted by the anxieties *in your head but with your present, loving heart.*

When you're playing Legos with Geo—which is really not your thing, but you do it because you love him—remember that when he's off at college, you'll miss these moments. Relish them. Rather than scarfing down dinner so you can answer emails, linger over Jamie's cooking long enough to actually acknowledge the thyme in the marinade. When you're writing, why not create something that doesn't dwell on drama, but, rather, acknowledges the moments you never write about: the good things.

Sincerely,
The version of yourself that is always accessible

JOURNALING PROMPTS

Address Your Wounds

What are the stressors that are consuming you in the following areas?

Weather/Environment:

Home:

Relationships:

Work/Passion Projects:

Channel Your Wisdom

What are the things you cherish in these same areas? They are reminders that stress is temporary.

Weather/Environment:

Home:

Relationships:

Work/Passion Projects:

Letter: Write a Remember Letter that you can read the next time life gets tough.

Date _____

Dear _____ ,

When _____ is bothering you because _____ , remember:

_____
_____
_____
_____
_____

When _____ is bothering you because _____ , remember:

_____
_____
_____
_____
_____

When _____ is bothering you because _____ , remember:

_____
_____
_____

When _____ is bothering you because _____ , remember:

You can always concentrate on the good stuff,
Your Optimistic Heart

P.S. Don't forget to read this back to yourself.

SECTION 2

Learning and Expanding

CHAPTER 8

Triage

On a sunny Saturday in March, I took Geo to a playdate at the park. As he chased his preschool friends around the slide, I caught up with one of the other moms. We stood in the woodchips and chatted about life, about the difficulties of juggling it all. She and her husband had been running their own business while raising their three daughters. On top of that, her husband had been temporarily transferred to D.C. for his other job.

"Last month, he was gone for three weeks and home for one," she said. "I kind of fell off the face of the earth." She shook her head, traumatized by the mere thought of it. "I never want to be separated like that again."

"I bet," I said. "You're just in pure survival mode."

"Exactly," she agreed. "It's triage."

It was such a fitting term that it stuck with me for the rest of the day.

Back home, while Geo zoomed his trucks around our living room floor, I thought about what happens in hospital triage. The nurse asks each incoming patient a list of questions to assess the severity of the situation, then prioritizes who gets treated first and how. The goal is to save as many people as possible.

Assess.

Prioritize.

Treat.

How accurate a metaphor for life. When we are in emergency situations, our needs inundate us, and we have to triage which ones are the most severe.

I always got into trouble when I didn't properly triage. Even when my psyche was internally bleeding—I felt disconnected from Jamie, I talked sharply to Geo, and I was bitter because I hadn't written in months—I concentrated my efforts on the thing that had a cold: my email inbox. When things got tough, I suddenly found it absolutely pertinent to organize my closet, unclog my pores, catch up on the latest reality TV, and search the internet for all-inclusive vacations.

Again and again, I did this, putting important conversations and rest on the backburner even when my soul was near death. It wasn't until I was barely functioning or my relationships were brittle that I paid attention.

It's because the symptoms are harder to see.

Sometimes, the loudest patient gets the drugs while the most suffering one quietly collapses in the corner.

At the hospital, the nurses use something that we rarely think to utilize: the check-in questionnaire. So often, that's the missing step in our lives—we don't take the minute we need for assessment. But over the past decade, I've been learning the hard way that it's imperative for us to take our own temperature, scan our bodies, and acknowledge what's hurting physically, mentally, emotionally, and spiritually. Then, once we have identified the problem, we must tend to our most bleeding wounds, even if it means taking time out of our busy lives. So often, we avoid care because we know that it will interrupt our schedules or take emotional effort. But, if a loved one was sick, wouldn't we give them medicine or get them to a doctor?

Then why do we avoid the very things that save us?

* * *

Everyone has their breakthrough moment, and this was mine: a beautiful Sunday afternoon in September, three years after moving back to Illinois. Sun streamed in through our kitchen windows. I should have been enjoying the day off of work and the quality time with my family, but I was so anxious that as Jamie and Geo lounged on the couch, I paced the house like a caged animal. The university hadn't renewed my teaching contract yet. Geo would be in kindergarten next year, and we wanted to buy a home in a good school system for him. Jamie hated his job, and Geo cried every morning at his daycare, leaving me to wonder if it was typical separation anxiety or if they were torturing him. Things were tipping toward catastrophe.

I was experiencing the kind of anxiety that ejects your soul from your body. You're physically there, but your mind and heart are on a high-speed rocket to planet panic. I couldn't hold my son or hug my husband because my own worry was so palpable that I felt like I was going to hyperventilate. I went for a walk to the nearby park—a place I loved so much. Its willow trees and brown-eyed susans usually calmed me, but not that day. Panic had won. I was the puppet, and fear was tugging the strings, manipulating my every thought and movement.

It made me feel both that I had no control—*something bad is going to happen, something bad is going to happen*—and that I had ultimate control: *If I'm hypervigilant enough and I constantly stand guard, I can prevent bad things from happening to my loved ones and me. I can get my boss to renew my contract. I can magically find a great house in a top school system. I can make Jamie happy. I can keep Geo safe.* Panic told me that the solution was easy: Don't eat. Don't sleep. Worry all the time.

It's simple, Panic said. *You can win the battle. All you have to do is give up being a present participant in your own life.*

Even in this prison, this solitary confinement, there was another voice. It was gentler, full of support and surrender: *You can't do this anymore, Sweetheart. Ask for help.*

How was it that, every week, I dedicated hours of my life to unloading the dishwasher and folding clothes, yet I designated zero time, beyond yoga class, to any other form of self-care? Was my own well-being not worth the hours?

I walked home and opened up to Jamie, and when I saw the concerned look in his eyes, I decided right then to make a change. I would put as much attention into healing myself as I put into the other areas of my life, and I would find someone to help me.

The following week, I entered a holistic health center for the first time. When my practitioner, Ann Baker, emerged to bring me back to her office, her presence struck me. She had a grey bob and hazel-grey eyes. It was immediately clear that she was a tender, wise soul. She wore flowy clothes and seemed to float as we headed down the hallway. Her "office" was a cozy nook that smelled of lavender oil.

I sunk into a comfy chair in the corner, took off my shoes, and sat cross-legged. Perched across from me, Ann led me through a grounding meditation and then asked what had brought me to her. She listened intently as I dumped out all of my life's woes. She breathed in slowly through her nose, and her whole body rose with the inhale. Then she exhaled deeply.

"It makes a case for mindfulness, doesn't it?" she said. "If we can't control the past or the future, then it makes experiencing the present moment really important."

"Truly," she added, "It's all we have: this moment. Now."

Her words heated my entire body, partly because I rarely lived in the moment. But the other part held hope because from then on, I could.

JOURNALING PROMPTS

Address Your Wounds

What worries are rocketing you to planet panic?

In which unsuccessful ways are you trying to control uncontrollable situations?

Channel Your Wisdom

Who or what helps lessen your panic?

What do you want to be present for in your life right now?

Treatment Plan: Write a treatment plan for yourself.

Date _____

Rank your health in each category from 1-10 and explain why you gave it that score.[2]

Mental:

_____
_____
_____
_____
_____
_____
_____

Emotional:

_____
_____
_____
_____
_____
_____
_____

---

[2] This four-part health assessment was inspired by a journaling exercise from Ann Baker. https://annpetrusbaker.com/

Spiritual:

___

Physical:

___

Let's triage. What doesn't need your attention right now? Which worries can you "Save the Date" on?

___

These three things need your attention the most right now:

1.
_____

_____

2.
_____

_____

3.
_____

_____

Create a treatment plan for healing.

_____

_____

_____

_____

_____

_____

CHAPTER 9

Try Again Politely

I stood in my university office with a stack of 100 ungraded student essays looming before me. My 330-page manuscript had to be proofread for the publisher. Though I'd made a rule to myself of no more than one nightly outing per week away from my family, I'd broken it and had committed myself to a faculty gathering, a creative writing gig, and a night out with friends. I'd had to cancel a session with my therapist because I was just too busy. My necessary seven hours of sleep became five. My temper became short. My outward appearance reflected it all—greasy hair with dark roots, a massive pimple on my right cheek, and red eyeballs from my dried-out contacts. But, worst of all, my tone with Geo and Jamie that week had been tense and annoyed.

How had it gotten to this? I had no time for the most important things.

But then I caught myself. I did have time, actually. I had 24 hours every day. It was that I hadn't *made* the time. We've all been guilty of this. Just the other day, a self-employed friend complained to me about being swamped with work.

"You should complain to your boss," I said, laughing.

Still, she continued, "I have a client every night this week and…"

"You make your own calendar, remember?" I said.

Had she forgotten that she was fully in charge of her time? I thought, and then a little nagging voice said, *Have we ALL forgotten that we're in charge of our time?*

Immediately, we defend ourselves because we have *this* and *this* and *this* to do. We feel tied to those commitments. But then we remember that we are the ones who signed our children up for multiple activities and that we *willingly volunteered* to host the potluck. It's hard to accept that we do, in fact, control our own schedules.

I used to pride myself on being busy. Anytime someone asked how I was, I'd say, *Ugh, SO busy!* Busy, busy, busy. I thought it meant I was important. It didn't. It meant I was overachieving, people-pleasing, and not prioritizing my own needs or those of my family.

There is a friend in our circle who never returns texts because she claims to be too busy. I used to get upset about it and compare my life to hers. *She thinks she's busy? She doesn't have half the responsibilities I do.* But when I got over the ego of it, I realized that the situation made me upset and sad because I registered as unimportant in her book. Her busyness was sending the message that I was a non-priority.

Since meeting with Ann, I was trying to use the word "busy" less because it implied that I hadn't prioritized my time. And when my schedule was overbooked, I was trying to own my part in it.

At my office, looking at the stack of 100 student essays, I realized that the answer to my own question "How had it gotten to this?" was simple: Because I had let it. Every decision had added up. Every. Single. One. The negative effect of how I'd started the week off that previous Sunday (not taking time for myself, not prepping meals, not scheduling my time appropriately) had rippled into the rest of the days. And that evening, I would have another night-time obligation, so I wouldn't be able to reconnect with myself or my family the way I needed to.

I messaged a good friend and typed, "I'm drowning."

In my mind, I could see the scenario: I was thrashing in the water. A large ship passed, making huge waves that pummeled me under the surface. My lungs were desperate for air. I felt the mighty weight and force of all the responsibilities I'd taken on, the things I "should" be doing. *I should go to that faculty meeting. I should stay at the university until all hours, working, I should go to a friend's gathering because she had come to mine, I should extend my office hours for that student. I should, I should, I should.* I tried to fight the waves, but I was working too hard, exerting myself, getting stressed out, and leaving no vitality for the most important things. There my family was, splashing near the shore, but I had no energy to get back to them. And I did it over and over again. I kept forgetting. And each time, it was harder to come back up for air.

Just as I was scolding myself for drowning (because it's always helpful to spend your energy yelling at yourself rather than, I don't know, saving your own life), a calm voice said, "Try again, politely."

It was a phrase I often used with Geo.

When he was bossy or cranky or downright rude, I'd simply say, "Try again, politely," and he'd have a second chance to express himself.

It had started one day when he marched into the kitchen and said, "Give me milk," as if I was his personal butler. When I didn't stop washing dishes that instant to pour him some 2%, he repeated the phrase like he was possessed. "Give me milk, givememilk, GIVEMEMILK!" I was about to say, "That's not how you ask for something," but instead, I simply rephrased it to be more positive, and I said three little words that made all the difference.

"Try again, politely."

It instantly clicked for him.

He batted his eyelashes and said, "May I have milk, please, Mama?"

It worked so well that I started using it for everything. If he threw his truck, I'd say, "Try again, politely," and he'd place it in his toy chest. If he was too rough with me, I'd say, "Try again, politely," and he'd embrace me.

I learned that the beauty of the second chance was that it usually produced the desired result. The other person just wasn't ready in the initial moment, so I allowed them another opportunity. It was easy enough to give second chances to friends and family, but I also needed to try again politely with myself. I had to offer myself second chances when I messed up (which was often) and when all the chatter in my head was negative (also often).

So, that morning in my office, as I mentally hissed at myself, "You shouldn't have overbooked your schedule. You shouldn't have been so short with Jamie and Geo," I simply said, "Try again, politely."

The thing about trying again politely is that it gives us permission to pause and reassess. It involves stillness and self-compassion, the two things we're most in need of.

I knew what I had to do. I opened up my laptop and logged into my Google calendar. Taking a deep breath, I clicked on that night's obligation, then pressed "Delete."

And there I was in my mind, coming up for air. This time, rather than thrashing, I simply turned onto my back and floated. Until I got enough energy to swim back to shore, I would rest and breathe.

"Keep floating," I told myself. "Just keep floating."

JOURNALING PROMPTS

Address Your Wounds

What does overwhelm look like in your life right now?

In what ways have you been shaming yourself?

Channel Your Wisdom

In which areas can you offer yourself a second chance? What can you change, stop, or do over right now?

What soothing words do you wish someone would say to you?

Self-Talk Transcript: Transcribe the hurtful things your brain tends to say.

Date _____

Negative Transcript

A few minutes of negative mind-chatter sounds like this:

_____

_____

_____

_____

_____

_____

_____

_____

_____

_____

_____

_____

_____

_____

Positive Transcript

Now write down what you would say in response to this negative chatter, as if you were giving your best friend a pep talk.

Here are the comforting things I want you to know, because you are the most important person in the world to me:

_____

_____

_____

_____

_____

_____

_____

_____

_____

_____

_____

_____

_____

Read this pep talk aloud to yourself.

CHAPTER 10

What Would Barbara Do?

It was the spring of 2017, and my memoir was about to be published. I was writing articles for magazines, sending the advanced reader copies to reviewers, working with my publicist, and planning a speaking tour. It was wonderfully amazing and, for the introvert in me, pretty overwhelming. Suddenly, there were a lot of rules: "You should organize your launch party like this. You need to post every day on social media. You should do book giveaways on Goodreads." Some of it felt forced. I wanted my book to reach readers, but I also wanted it to feel authentic. When I finally got fed up, I paused and asked myself: *What would Barbara do?*

Jamie and I met Barbara on our honeymoon in Italy. We'd asked a travel agent acquaintance to find a tour for us, and she'd secured an all-inclusive, weeklong getaway to the Italian lakes for a steal. We'd never been on a vacation like that before and were shocked to find something in our budget. We jumped at the opportunity, and I fantasized about us holding hands, adventuring around Europe, and meeting other fun travelers. My friends had just come back from their honeymoon, where they'd met other newlyweds and hung out all week, going on hikes and having dinners together. I imagined our trip to be like that.

After our flight to Italy, we entered the dim hotel banquet room to meet our adventurous tour group and found tables of diners in their 70s and 80s.

"I think we're in the wrong room," I whispered to Jamie.

But no, there was a sign for Cosmos, our tour company. Our guide showed us to our seats and started her welcome speech. Jamie and I exchanged glances and politely listened to her opening remarks, all the while wondering how we could get ahold of our travel agent to change our tour. The other guests seemed lovely enough, but the vibe didn't exactly match the exciting, romantic honeymoon we'd envisioned. When the gnocchi was served, I looked around, hoping I'd missed another set of newlyweds, but found none. My fantasies of clinking glasses with other honeymooners concluded just as early as our evening, and we went to bed at nine.

The next day, our "walking" tour was mostly driving around in the tour bus, and I was grumpy, itching for adventure. But that night at dinner, we sat at a new table to meet some of the other tour guests, and my perspective started to shift a bit. That's when we met a firecracker in her 70s named Barbara who downed espressos and merlot like it was her job. Next, we introduced ourselves to another couple who was not, in fact, retired but on the third week of their six-week holiday, since Europe offered their employees much better benefits than American companies. The last couple at the table—two women from England—had us slapping our knees as they roasted me for my Midwestern accent. Everything I said sounded like a joke to them, and they'd constantly ask, "Are you taking the piss?" That evening, Jamie and I went to bed at midnight, our bellies sore from laughing.

With each passing day at Lake Como and Maggiore, our tour group got rowdier, bursting into spontaneous song, laughing hard, and playing pranks on each other. We became closer with Barbara, the couple on holiday, and the English wives. As our vacation drew to a close, I knew I'd miss them when we returned to Massachusetts.

During our last dinner together, we sat around, exchanging contact information, when Barbara passed out her business card. I was about to put it in my wallet when the picture on it caught my attention—an image of a buffalo. The buffalo grazed in a green field under the words "Barbara's Buffalo Grooming." The rest of the dinner table noticed it too, and we were all quiet for a minute, trying to figure out the logistics. *Wasn't the buffalo population previously endangered? Were there actually buffalo owners who wanted their herds closely cropped and sharply shaven? And once the haircut requests came in, how did someone actually groom a buffalo?* We cautiously asked our questions, trying desperately not to offend Barbara or hint that this didn't seem like a lucrative business model. How could this woman travel the world on her meager buffalo-grooming salary? Barbara listened patiently to our questions, and then, slowly, a smile spread across her face, and she laughed so hard she almost spit out her wine.

"It's a joke," she said. We all looked at each other, confused.

"I had these cards made up for fun," she said, wiping the laughter tears from the corner of her eyes. "This is priceless," she added. "You should see your faces right now."

Realizing we'd all been duped, we slapped our palms onto the table, laughing until we couldn't catch our breath. I was in awe of her wit. This woman possessed the imagination to not only think up a fake profession but then she had gone to great lengths to design and print the cards. She was one of the most unpredictable women I'd ever met. She stood apart from the herd, like the lone buffalo on her faux business card. The next day, when we got on the plane to head back to our predictably planned lives, I took out Barbara's business card and smiled at it.

I'd hold on to it in the years to come, when I traveled alone to El Salvador, when we put our rural Massachusetts house up for sale and moved to Chicago with baby Geo, when I decided to write a book during his infancy, and now, as I prepped for the release of my memoir. I wanted my choices to emanate Barbara's fun-loving, unpredictable personality. So I asked myself, "What would make this publishing season adventurous and whimsical?" To start, I insisted on changing my book cover's design to be more colorful—a hot pink spine and a vibrant print around the summary. Then, I decided to turn my book tour into a family road trip. Since most of the conferences I was presenting at provided airfare and lodging, my loved ones could join me on the cheap. Jamie and Geo would accompany me to Pennsylvania and Massachusetts, Mom to Oregon, and Dana to Mexico. I decided to hold local events at my favorite bookstores and yoga studios. I asked all of my friends and family to be a part of the experience, and boy, did they rise to the occasion. Jamie had a nine-foot retractable sign of my book cover made to take to events. My catering friend signed up to provide the food at one of my launches. Dana, her boyfriend, and Mom entertained Geo in the nooks of bookstores while I presented.

And on the day my book came out, I chose my favorite meeting room on my university's campus, overlooking Lake Michigan, to hold the book launch party. I invited everyone I'd taught over the years and the professors who'd supported me. My lovely director provided a yummy spread, and Jamie left work early to help me haul my signs and books to the top-floor meeting room. But once we set everything up and people started streaming in, I ran to the bathroom and hid. My nerves shook. This room had hosted such literary greats as Mary Karr, and soon, all of the most brilliant professors I knew would be taking seats to hear me speak. I felt the overwhelming expectation to be intelligent and academic. But then I thought of Barbara. What would feel fun and authentic to me?

I went back out to the room—full of all those smart people—and I cranked dance songs over the loudspeakers. I let out a happy sigh, and people shimmied as they found their seats. I went row by row and greeted my former students and my beloved colleagues, thanking them for attending. Then, instead of starting the event with a long stuffy reading, as was the norm at these gatherings, I told the story of the winding, unpredictable road that had led me to becoming a writer. And I felt Barbara's presence with me, indeed.

JOURNALING PROMPTS

Address Your Wounds

What are the ruts or patterns you've fallen into that don't feel authentic to you?

What stops you from having fun or being playful?

What are the responsibilities you're carrying?

Channel Your Wisdom

What does fun look like to you? Who or what makes you laugh? What have you done in the past to play?

When was the last time you surprised yourself or others by doing something unpredictable?

How can you incorporate more play and whimsy and laughter into your life?

Permission Slip: Write yourself a permission slip to play.

Date _____

I give permission for _____ *(your name) to participate in the following adventures, pranks, laughter, and general silliness:*

_____

_____

_____

_____

_____

_____

_____

_____

_____

_____

_____

_____

_____

_____

These activities must be completed on or by the following dates:

Your Signature Here

CHAPTER 11

Nature Lessons

We bought a home in Northern Illinois the winter before Geo entered kindergarten. Just as I'd heard the whisperings when it was time to move to the city, I heard the same whisperings when it was time to move out. Chicago had been good to us, but we'd had our fill and were ready for less noise, less traffic, and less congestion. We'd chosen the home because of its school district, which had a dual language program where Geo would learn in Spanish for half the day and English for the other. But we'd also chosen it because it was on a little lake.

When the first spring came to our new yard, it did not disappoint. As soon as the snow melted, it became clear that our neighborhood was a nature corridor. Our lake took the shape of an S, and our house was nestled in the upper bend, so we got a semi-circular view of it all—the sky, the willows, the water. And our spot on the lake seemed to be the landing strip for all of the geese and ducks.

Every spring morning, as I cracked eggs into the pan for some over-easies, I looked out the kitchen window for my swimming and flying friends to see what they were up to and to witness their little rituals. One morning, Jamie and I watched the ducks. Their webbed feet and tail feathers went up in the air when they dove underwater for food. When they bathed, they plunked their heads under the little waves, resurfaced, and shimmied the droplets down their backs. Next, they raised themselves out of the water to flap their wings a couple times, drying off. I found it all incredibly fascinating since I'd never had a front-row seat to nature like this before.

And our lake had a usual crew that stuck to a routine we could set a clock to—four sets of Canada geese, a bunch of mallards, and two white ducks that the neighbor across the lake raised himself. They seemed to rest and waddle and swim and graze at the same time every day.

One morning, a pair of our usual geese swam by, but in between them was a line of six tiny, fuzzy goslings. I spent the better part of an hour just watching them and wondering about so many things: *How were they already able to swim? How did they know to stay behind one parent and in front of the other, in a line? How were they taught, when they went up onto the grassy shore, to stay away from the street?*

I started meditating in one of our red lawn chairs in the morning, and afterward, I'd watch the geese. Then I'd close my eyes and listen to the sound of the mourning doves and finches who hung out in our river birch tree. There was another type of bird

I'd never noticed before moving to our new house—a blackbird with neon coral shoulders—and I found out after a Google search that they're called red-winged blackbirds. We had slews of them, and they whistled and trilled and let out an o-ka-lee sound.

One such red-winged blackbird always returned to our feeder, even when we were nearby. He was comfortable in our presence, and Geo named him Squawky. The geese and ducks and birds became our feathered companions. We looked for them every day and loved seeing what they were up to. They understood all the important things about life. It was simple, really. Their communication said it all. Squawky had about five sounds: one for greeting other birds, one for attracting a mate, one for guarding territory, one for telling others that there was food, and one for alerting others that there was a predator. And the ducks were no-nonsense as well. If they didn't want another duck nearby, they darted at it till it got the message. The geese, too, were straightforward, honking their arrival and departure and standing guard when their babies grazed.

There was no BS.

Also, this was their territory, and we were the spectators. It's like they were looking at all of us humans, shaking their heads, saying, *Watch and learn, you fools. Stop getting caught up in all the chaos. What's important here is finding a partner, searching for food, protecting your family, and having a good swim or flight in the meantime.*

Geo was learning lessons too, but from the fish, not the birds.

He and Jamie started fishing off of our little dock on Sunday afternoons as the sun set before us, displaying its vibrant pinks like a watercolor painting behind our lake. We usually listened to Fleetwood Mac from our portable speaker, and, almost always, a delicious smoky smell wafted over from our grill. Jamie and Geo did catch and release, and though they'd seen big bass in the lake, they'd only caught a sunfish. But we were trying to teach Geo that fishing was about much more than what he caught. I loved watching his and Jamie's comfortable silence as they cast and reeled, cast and reeled, watching the water, all their senses heightened.

One Sunday, while Geo fished, Jamie and I put our arms around each others' backs as we stood on the dock to watch him. He cast his Paw Patrol fishing pole, again and again, too impatient to let the bobber hang out for long. We got splattered with lake water as Geo flung his pole around. Jamie and I smiled and silently giggled because no matter how many times we told him to face his body toward the lake instead of the house, he didn't listen, and often, the hook landed on the shore rocks, not in the water.

When he got upset, he said, "That wasn't a good cast."

"What if you told yourself that you'll try again?" I asked.

At first, he resisted, but then he started smiling, reeling the line back in and saying, "I'll try again."

When dusk turned the sky pink and Geo still hadn't caught a fish, he got upset.

"But we didn't catch anything," he whined.

So Jamie and I asked, "Buddy, what is fishing about?" and Geo recited, with an eye-roll, "About spending time in nature with the people you love."

"Exactly," I said.

Geo rolled his eyes again. But later that evening, when I turned on his star night light and tucked him into bed, he said, "Guess what, Mom?"

"What, Boo Bear?" I asked.

"I had a lot of fun today. Even though I didn't catch a fish."

And I realized in that moment that, essentially, our backyard was teaching him everything he needed to know about life.

JOURNALING PROMPTS

Address Your Wounds

What nature and animals are you desperately yearning to see?

How have your surroundings impacted you in the past?

Channel Your Wisdom

How are your current surroundings impacting you now?

What can you learn from watching nature and animals?

Seasonal Plan: How can you live more in tune with nature and the seasons, scheduling your routine according to the time cycles and energy of the season? Below, write down the shifts or choices you can make in each category according to the seasons.

Date _____

Summer:

Routine/Rhythms:

Activities:

Seasonal Foods:

Attire:

Energy:

Introspection:

Fall:

Routines/Rhythms:

Activities:

Seasonal Foods:

Attire:

Energy:

Introspection:

Winter:

Routine/Rhythms:

Activities:

Seasonal Foods:

Attire:

Energy:

Introspection:

Spring:

Routines/Rhythms:

Activities:

Seasonal Foods:

Attire:

Energy:

Introspection:

CHAPTER 12

Witnessing

I realized one morning while journaling that much of my growth happened outside the house. I wrote at coffee shops and did yoga at a studio. I sent thoughtful texts and emails while at my office. But I'd tried so hard to separate work from home life so that Geo could get my full attention that he wasn't getting to see some of the best parts of me. Much of my kindness and creativity were invisible to him because they didn't happen in front of him.

One of the most essential questions I started asking myself was: *What do I want Geo to see? What do I want him to witness about me?* It helped me realize that we have a lot of input over other people's impressions of us, not just by how we interact with them but by what we do in front of them. So I sat down and thought about the things I wanted Geo to see me doing.

I wanted him to see me being kind to other people.

I wanted him to see me being mindful and grateful.

I wanted him to see me creating—painting, making jewelry, journaling.

So, one night, I pulled out my jewelry-making kit—something I hadn't touched in a few years. It was filled with beads from old necklaces and earrings that I could repurpose to make something new. As I spread out my supplies, Geo was all about it. He loved using different pliers to cut and shape the wire, then stringing the beads. And he combined it with an act of kindness—he made necklaces and earrings for me, Grandma, and Auntie.

It made me realize that the question "What do I want others to witness?" is important.

What did I want Jamie to witness? My friends? My students? My neighbors? What did I want to witness about myself?

As soon as I asked this question, the answer popped into my brain fully formed: *Being kind to myself. Taking care of myself.*

I made a list of things that acted as preventative maintenance for my well-being, things that reduced the likelihood of illness or injury to my psyche. I'd once heard a wellness coach describe them as "non-negotiables," and it had stayed with me. I liked the concreteness of it, the "no exceptions" mentality, like, maybe, just maybe, our own self-care was important enough to take seriously.

My list included seven hours of sleep, healthy food, vitamins, regular therapy appointments, slow breathing, quality time with loved ones, journaling, walking, and yoga. And just when my perfectionist brain said, in its militant tone, *You must do all those things every single day so that you can stay in control and never suffer again*, my wiser self, witnessing this charade, tapped me on the shoulder and said, *Just to let you know, it doesn't really work like that. Something may come up that might interrupt your perfect plan—Geo might get a fever, and there goes your night of sleep. Winter may come again—it's got a good track record of showing up every year—and you might be too socked in by snow to go for a walk. So, let's try our best to do these things as often as possible because they make you really centered, but you know what you need most when things don't go as expected? Do you know what Geo needs to witness you giving yourself in your hardest moments?*

I nodded because I already knew the answer.

Then I wrote SELF-COMPASSION, in all caps, on my list.

JOURNALING PROMPTS

Address Your Wounds

What are some of your qualities or behaviors that you don't like others to witness?

Why?

Channel Your Wisdom

What are your best qualities or behaviors that you want other people to witness?

How can you make those qualities more visible?

List: Write a list of your non-negotiables.

Date _____

Your non-negotiables:

1 _____

2 _____

3 _____

4 _____

5 _____

6 _____

7 _____

8 _____

9 _____

10 _____

Remember that life intervenes, and sometimes we need to be flexible. Create a backup plan for being gentle and tender to yourself in the midst of life obstacles. What are tiny things you can do to feel better if life throws you for a loop?

CHAPTER 13

Trampoline Savasana

Geo entered kindergarten in the fall of 2018. That first day of school, I almost walked onto the bus with him, but Jamie put his hand on my shoulder and gently whispered, "He can do it, Mama."

But how would he carry that heavy backpack? Would he make friends with his seatmate? Would he be safe on the bus without a seat belt? Once at school, would he find his way to his classroom? Would he feel overwhelmed by learning in Spanish for half of the day? Would the afternoon bus driver know where to stop? So went my worries, but mostly the question behind them was: *When did he get so big? How had the baby who had grown in my womb become a five-year-old boy who was heading off to school without me?*

As the bus pulled away, I waved and waved, blowing kisses long after the taillights had disappeared. And then I sobbed into Jamie's chest. *It had all gone by too fast.* I knew Geo needed to test his independence, but how could I let go?

His entering kindergarten inspired another letting go too. I understood that I wanted to be with Geo after school in the afternoons, so I talked to my department and asked to teach all my classes earlier in the day, so I could leave by 2:30 and be home to get Geo off the bus. Sure, it meant very early days on Mondays, Wednesdays, and Fridays and doing grading at home instead of at the office, but it also helped me loosen my grip on the idea that I needed to keep proving myself at work. I had to be content with the fact that even if I was not the first one in and the last one out, I was still a valuable colleague. My evaluations showed it. I figured this: I could spend a lifetime at the university, but I'd never get back this time with my son. It was weird at first when coworkers said, "I feel like I rarely see you these days. I was so used to you living at the office." My shame alarm went off: *Not enough, not enough, not enough.* But, no, I was reducing a ridiculous work schedule to a normal one, and I was still a worthy employee. So I said, "I leave early now to get Geo off the bus, and I love it."

And there I was, at the bus stop every afternoon, smiling like crazy, waving frantically. When the door folded open, Geo would jump from the top step and leap into my arms, and I'd smother him with kisses. Then I'd take his heavy backpack off, hold his hand, and we'd make our way to our house to sit on the front porch for a snack and interesting conversations. Under the shade of our river birch tree, as the birds chirped, Geo would say things like:

Do you know that dung beetles collect poop?

I think we should cook minnows for Thanksgiving.
Do dentists have teeth?
How do turtles communicate?
Mom, for your birthday, I'm going to give you a toy I don't play with anymore.
Do you think that Sour Patch Kids taste like sausage?
If I have my humidifier on at night, how can I dream?
Mom, if you break your windshield, you should call 1-800-FELDCO.

Then one day, we had an interesting spiritual conversation, completely initiated by Geo when he asked me, "Mom, what are angels?"

I paused for a second, thinking of the simplest explanation. I said, "Some people believe they're invisible things that protect us."

"From what?" he asked.

"From bad things," I said, afraid that I'd opened up a can of worms about all the horrible tragedies in the world, like abuse and crime. But he said, "Oh like, from cheetahs?"

"Yeah, like from cheetahs," I said, laughing inside.

After a snack and some downtime, Geo and I would go to the backyard and climb up the ladder to the trampoline. We'd sit on the ledge and peel off our socks and shoes. Then he'd unzip the netting, and in we would go for a half hour of jumping. This ritual belonged to the two of us alone, and even the placement of the trampoline in our yard felt intimate—our tree created a canopy of shade so that the bouncy black mesh was cold under our feet. The lake and the willow trees were our backdrop. As soon as we'd climb in, we'd begin a beautiful, sometimes silent dance between mother and son. We'd leap in circles, weaving in and out of each other's paths. Then, sweaty, panting, warmed-up, we'd start to giggle. We'd squeal in delight, make our way to the middle, and play popcorn. I'd bounce next to Geo and catapult him up into the air. We'd do the splits mid-jump. We'd do karate kicks and grab a rubber ball for a game of dodgeball. I'd have his full attention, and he'd have mine. There were no toys or emails distracting us from each other. Then the smell of tacos would waft from the open kitchen window, and Jamie would call out, "Dinner's ready." Geo and I would slow our steps. We'd gravitate toward the center, holding each others' hands for our favorite game, where we'd spin in circles with our eyes closed until we were laughing and dizzy. Then we'd plop down, sighing and rolling onto our backs to take a one-minute savasana on the mesh. I'd point out the clouds above us, and we'd listen to the birds chatter, but mentally, I'd say thank you to the universe—for 30 minutes of youthful joy, 30 minutes of mindful jumping, 30 minutes of bliss with my beautiful boy.

I wouldn't have traded any of those afternoons with Geo for time at my office.

JOURNALING PROMPTS

Address Your Wounds

Who or what is getting more of your attention than you'd like?

What are you afraid would happen if you gave less of your energy/attention to those people and things?

Channel Your Wisdom

Write down your obligations during a typical week. Does this reflect the things you hold most dear? If it doesn't, how can you adjust your schedule to give more time to yourself and the people you love?

What are the simple sacred rituals you can create daily or weekly to preserve together time?

Sacred activities aren't always additional things you have to add to your calendar. What are you already doing together that you can give more meaning to?

Calendar: Write down the schedule you want to have. Include regular connection time with yourself and others.

	Morning	Afternoon	Evening
Mon			
Tues			
Wed			
Thur			
Fri			
Sat			
Sun			

CHAPTER 14

Noticing Walks

On Tuesday and Thursday mornings when Geo was in first grade, I started going for sunrise walks. Jillian Michaels wasn't happy about it. That's what Jamie calls the drill sergeant part of me who thought I needed to go for a five-mile jog when I had the flu. Jillian did not believe in strolling through the neighborhood and noticing the leaves. But on Tuesday and Thursday, I started "sleeping in" until 6:15 (oh, if my college-self only knew that I'd one day consider this a treat).

It was usually still dark as I wrapped my arms around Jamie's warm body and nuzzled into his neck. After a good snuggle, I threw a coat over my pajamas and slipped on my boots; then, I was out the door. The October air was crisp, in the 50s, and it woke up my lungs as I breathed it in. I inhaled the sweet smell of the dried grass. The leaves crunched under my boots. As I walked around the lake, I took lots of deep breaths, and then I began my mental conversation with the universe. It always started with "Thank you." My gratitude list was long and usually included sunshine, people, food, acts of kindness, and opportunities that had come my way. Then I talked about anything that was troubling me—something triggering from my past or something unknown about my future.

"I'm open to your guidance," I'd say. "I'm listening."

I kept walking and tried to reduce the mental chatter to make room for silence.

One morning, during a sunrise walk, I said, "Tell me what I need to know," and then I waited.

Breaking the silence, a voice spoke back, sounding like my voice but wiser, all-knowing.

"You don't need to *know* anything," it said. "You just need to *notice*."

It was so simple, so obvious, yet so profound. And I did notice—a sparkly, foggy mist hovered above the lake, and the sun shone like glitter on the water. The beauty around me was breathtaking. The tips of the leaves blazed red, and I wanted to knock on doors and say, "Have you *seen* this maple tree? My god, it's gorgeous."

During another walk, I yearned to travel. It was an ache always deep within me, and sometimes I felt weighed down by responsibility and practicality. I wanted Jamie, Geo, and I to wander the world. But there's this little thing called "school" and this other little thing called "work" that were kind of important. So, I was lamenting a bit, and I offered it up. The universe spoke back right away, sounding very certain.

"You'll have your wandering time," it said. "But when you do, you'll always be searching for stability, so live this settled life now and cherish it while you have it."

The voice was so spot on, and I knew it to be true. I was positive that our future would include travel, but I also remembered my younger self, who had less responsibility and could traverse the globe but was always searching for a cozy space and person to come home to. It's so cliché, "the grass is always greener" mentality: When I'm wandering, my heart yearns for home-cooked dinners and familiar routines, and when I'm at home, my heart yearns for the adventure of wandering. Here I was, with the cozy home and the family I'd always wanted. I needed to cherish them.

Another time, when I was overcome with terror about the world my son was growing up in—the corruption, the crime, the bullies, the hate, the environmental collapse—I simply said, *Alright, universe. Help me, please. I can't handle this. This is beyond me.*

The famous pastor Rob Bell says that a lot of his prayers are, "*Here, you take it.*"[3] I adopted this too. I imagined myself handing over whatever hardship was just too big or out of my control to figure out, and I'd say, *Here you go, take this.* Sometimes I'd touch the trunk of a tree I was passing, hoping that it could absorb the tension in my soul, like carbon dioxide, and turn it into life-sustaining oxygen.

Then I'd sigh, feeling the release of surrender.

One day on a noticing walk, I saw a cardinal looking down at me, and I realized something. Maybe I wasn't just walking to notice. Maybe I was walking to *be* noticed—to be seen, to be heard. Just as I was looking at the beauty of creation all around me, maybe it was looking right back at me with the same awe.

These profound moments of insight shocked me, but what's most amazing is that it's always accessible—for me, for all of us. It's right there, inside our souls.

All we have to do is still our minds and listen.

We just have to notice.

And we're home.

---

3   Bell, "Is Your Best Day Behind You?"

JOURNALING PROMPTS

Address Your Wounds

What can you offer up to the universe and say, *Here, take this?*

Channel Your Wisdom

What is your heart asking you to pay attention to?

When the universe looks at you, what does it see?

Dialogue

Go for a noticing walk or look out your window for a few minutes. Have a dialogue with the universe or your wise self. Ask her your questions, and see what she says. Write down your conversation.

You:

_____

_____

_____

Universe:

_____

_____

_____

You:

_____

_____

_____

Universe:

You:

Universe:

You:

Universe:

You:

Universe:

SECTION 3

Dealing and Healing When Life Doesn't Go As Planned

CHAPTER 15

Fierce

On a chilly March day in 2020, I paced my kitchen as everything shut down around us—my university, Jamie's company, Geo's school, and my usually-open heart. As the virus spread, so did my sadness and panic. Nowhere felt safe, especially given that I taught in Chicago, where cases were soaring. The future had never felt so uncertain, but I'd long ago learned that certainty is the greatest of illusions. In fact, remembering this actually helped me breathe a bit. It's true we never know what might happen in the next second, but we do have the present moment and the gift of tender self-talk. So, in the midst of worrying about my hospital-worker mom and troubleshooting how I'd teach remote courses while helping Jamie homeschool first-grade lessons to Geo, I put my worries on pause to go for a drive, then I came back and journaled. Here's what surfaced.

Oh, Fearful Heart,

Lately, with everything going on in the world, you've forgotten something important, Mama: You are FIERCE. As you go for a drive on a gray March Sunday, Sia comes on, and, man, something comes through you. No, something comes from within you. Sia is singing about "a bird set free," and you crank up the knob to the highest volume, singing off-key.[4] You belt it. Top of the lungs, no breath-catching. You bob your head; you drum the wheel; you want to go 100 on the highway because you feel this uncontainable thing inside of you that just wants to be let loose.

You are so sick of being afraid. Worry and fear make you feel so unbearably fragile, and though you'd never describe yourself as a small being, you realize that worry makes you think and act from such a shrunken place. But there's something about that Sia song that unearths vibrations from deep inside of you, and there it is—you feel it in your throaty belting. You are SO freaking fierce. Here's how you know that it's not a lie: You have proof, evidence, and example after example of times your sheer force could have shaken the Earth.

You are so fierce that you left everything and everyone you knew for a fresh start, a new beginning, growth, and change. You proved to yourself that you could do it. You could make your mark, even in unfamiliar territory.

---

4   Sia, "Bird Set Free"

You are so fierce that when you met your partner and felt what love truly was, you ignored what people might say about age or distance, and you took one step forward and then another until your lives intertwined. And now you've been together for almost two decades.

You are so fierce that you told truths people did not want to hear because even though it upset the status quo, it freed your spirit, and you didn't have to hold that poison in anymore.

You are so fierce that you let go of toxic relationships. While that meant you were sometimes lonely, you stood in your integrity, which is the best company of all.

You are so fierce that you took Mary Oliver's advice, which says: "You do not have to be good. You do not have to walk on your knees for a hundred miles through the desert repenting."[5]

You are so fierce that you forgave yourself time and time again.

You are so fierce that, in the hardest of situations, an eerie calm came over you, and you stepped up. You handled it. While everything was falling apart, you became the steady force.

You are so fierce that when you were in the depths of despair, you did the fiercest thing of all: You had faith in the universe, and you let go.

You are so fierce that when you needed to fall apart, you allowed yourself to do so, and you asked for help. Because you knew that falling apart meant you could build yourself anew.

You are so fierce that when you heard bad news, you refused to believe in any other future besides the one where everything would be alright.

You are so fierce that you labored and birthed. You rode those painful waves, and the warrior within you took over as you bore witness to a magnificent miracle.

You are so fierce that when you felt undeniable love for your child and you were terrified of everything in the entire world that could hurt him, you kept breathing, kept holding on, and kept talking to yourself so that you could be present even in the midst of your terror.

You are so fierce that you dealt with all of life's major stressors again and again. So much heartache and loss could ruin a person. But you pushed and paused and pushed and paused until it finally passed, and you were still standing.

You are so fierce that you put yourself out there for interviews, promotions, raises, and opportunities. You asked and asked and asked. You always said, "Why not me?" You told yourself that nothing is unattainable. You spoke up, Mama. And the universe answered back, giving you opportunities beyond your wildest dreams, all because you had the confidence to ask.

You are so fierce that you put your most vulnerable stories out there for the world

---

5 Oliver, *Dream Work*

to see, and you stood in that truth unapologetically. You knew that people might connect or they might judge; it wasn't under your control. You put your words out there anyway.

You are so fierce that you had hundreds of hard conversations with your partner, from the little annoyances and the saddest sorrows to the deepest desires. You brought them up; you put them out there. You did not sweep them under the rug. You did not bite your tongue. You did not succumb to embarrassment. You held hands; you cried; you sat in rage and sadness, in sorrow and regret, in unabashed love. Together. And, each time, you grew stronger as partners.

You are so fierce that you handled your reactions at times when people were acting foolish. You realized it wasn't about you. Their stuff was not yours to own.

You are so fierce that you have tested the bounds of your body—you've hiked, climbed, balanced, run, lifted, and loved, feeling every fiber in your muscles respond with the pride and wonder of what your beautiful body can do.

You are so fierce that you have resisted deprivation and exhaustion. Instead, you have rested and nourished your body and soul.

You are so fierce that you've embraced fun—skipping and splashing, jumping and dancing, laughing and playing. You are worthy of a life of enjoyment.

You are so fierce that you have supported other women—empowered them, lifted them up—because there is room for all of our glorious gifts, and we are better when we collaborate.

And the fiercest thing you've done? You've sung your song. You hugged your child tight. You've stared into your partner's eyes. You've apologized. You've had so much freaking self-compassion. You have loved SO hard. And now, when you're so sick of feeling small, you're reminded that you haven't been small a single day in your life, Mama. You were born fierce. You have defied every misconception. There is such a fire inside you that those who test it feel the force and know not to tread any further. Today, you just needed a reminder. Fear needed a reminder. So you roll down your window, let the cold air in, flip the bird to it all—the terror, the worry. And you "shout it out, like a bird set free."[6]

Always here to remind you,
Your Fierce Heart

6   Sia, "Bird Set Free"

JOURNALING PROMPTS

Address Your Wounds

What is making you feel small and scared?

What fear stories are playing through your mind?

Channel Your Wisdom

What does "fierce" look like to you?

Who are your fierce mentors?

Write a FIERCE playlist: What are your favorite fierce songs, books, movies, podcasts, and outfits?

Bonus Activities: Crank your favorite fierce tunes and dance your heart out by yourself. Close the door and your eyes if you need to, whatever will help you feel uninhibited. Or go for a drive and belt your favorite tunes at the top of your lungs.

Exercise: Write your fierce rally cry, reminding yourself why you're SO fierce.

Date _____

YOU ARE FIERCE

What a powerhouse you are! Here are all the ways you've demonstrated your fierceness in life. You are so fierce that:

_____

_____

_____

_____

_____

_____

Here are all the ways you've demonstrated your fierceness in love. You are so fierce that:

_____

_____

_____

_____

_____

_____

_____

Here are all the ways you've demonstrated your fierceness by standing in your integrity. You are so fierce that:

_____

_____

_____

_____

_____

_____

_____

_____

Today, you'll be fierce by:

_____

_____

_____

_____

_____

_____

You've never been small a day in your life!
Your Fierce Heart

P.S. Read this aloud to yourself in your most powerful voice.

CHAPTER 16
Finding Joy in Hidden Places

My sister is a master champion of Easter egg hunts.

While others may think of them as a delightful activity for kids to frolic in fields of colored eggs, she views them as an all-out battle, a testament of brute strength against her opponent—that opponent being, well, me. And before it seems like I'm digging up buried beefs from our childhood, it's important to know that to this very day, we still duke it out over Easter eggs. But even though she beats me every single time, I love these egg hunts with my sister.

You see, ever since we were little, egg hunts have been the main event of the Easter holiday. As soon as we fell asleep, our parents would hide dozens of eggs all around the house. Well, *hide* is an understatement. They would expertly color-coordinate the eggs to camouflage with their surroundings, like a green egg nestled in a houseplant or a red egg inside a red vase. There were eggs in utensil drawers, eggs in couch corners, eggs in shower caddies, and eggs in pantry nooks.

As soon as Dana and I woke up, we would grab our bunny baskets, and my parents would stand back as an all-out brawl began. Dana would throw out elbow jabs and hip checks, anything to get me out of the way so she could get the egg. Mind you, these eggs held jelly beans and quarters, not some coveted prize. Still, there would be yells and shrieks, and I'd fight back, grabbing onto Dana's arm or leg to stop her. And while I am strong, I am not as strong as her, so I would run the other way and go for hiding spots she hadn't investigated yet. Soon, she'd catch on, and she'd chase after me. Cue more elbow jabs and hip checks back and forth, both of us laughing all the while. Our parents would stand back, watching the mayhem unfold. Sometimes the egg would be right there, beneath our very noses, and yet we wouldn't see it, so they'd say "Warm, warmer, hot, hotter" until we saw what was there all along.

The thing is that this tradition has never stopped. When Dana morphed from a little kid to a soccer star in high school, we still did egg hunts. When she was home from college and I was visiting from Massachusetts, we still did egg hunts. As Dana worked her way through graduate school and became an impactful social worker, we still did egg hunts. Those fun battles became the backdrop of Dana morphing from my little sister into my best friend. And then Geo was born, and I watched Dana morph, once again, into the most loving, caring auntie. I'll never forget when Geo was six months old, and Jamie and Geo and I all came down with what we thought was food poisoning, and we couldn't take care of ourselves, let alone each other. Dana flew to Massachusetts on her non-existent, fresh-out-of-college budget to take care of Geo. As a thank you, we gave her what turned out to be a contagious stomach bug, and she puked the whole plane ride home.

When Geo became a toddler, he loved helping me hide eggs for his auntie to find, except he liked to walk behind her during the hunt to reach into her basket and steal all her jelly beans. Then, when Dana met her boyfriend, he quickly folded into the family dynamic. He loves festivities and a themed party, possibly more than anyone we know. He wears matching holiday socks and dyes Easter eggs every year, so he didn't even blink when he witnessed his new girlfriend and her sister fight to the death over plastic eggs.

Easter is now one of our favorite holidays to spend together as a family, where there are multiple rounds of egg hunts so that everybody gets a chance to hide and find. It's about the mystery of the hiding spot, the excitement of the unknown, the laughing and pushing each other out of the way like when we were kids. But I think it's really about the excuse to play.

And, during the pandemic, we needed laughter and play and fun more than ever. In addition to the tragic injustices and unimaginable losses, the loneliness was so pervasive.

I desperately missed hugging my mom and sister. I missed hanging out with them and friends inside without masks. I missed watching Geo, who'd been e-learning since March, get on a school bus and play with friends carefree. I missed being able to care intimately for relatives with serious non-COVID health issues. I missed our East Coast community and watching the joy spread across Jamie's face when he visited his family.

And, of course, I missed the small things that actually didn't seem so small anymore—going to coffee shops and writing there all day, rolling out my mat at my local yoga studio, booking a babysitter and having date night with Jamie, having our usual Easter celebration. I missed living a life where I wasn't always worried about getting or giving the virus.

And yet, there was still joy to be found. In drive-by birthday parades, in receiving flowers on my doorsteps from neighbors, in exchanging Easter and Mother's Day gifts outside with Mom and Dana—our eyes crinkling with joy above our masks. In fact, that entire spring and summer, we found joy in the most camouflaged of places—in outdoor picnics with my family, in listening to Brothers Osborne and dancing around the kitchen with Geo as Jamie sautéed spinach and garlic, in taking walks with friends around the lake path in Evanston, in sitting quietly and listening to my heart beating rhythmically inside my chest.

At first, it seems that bliss is nowhere to be found, and then you see it hidden everywhere—tucked into a couch corner, nestled in a plant. There and there and there. The little joys are everywhere. And because we've had to jostle and wrestle our way through hardships in order to notice them, it makes them all the sweeter. While I think there's happiness in the opening of them to see what's inside, the true bliss is in the finding: in realizing that they've been there all along, right beneath our very noses, waiting for us to discover them.

JOURNAL PROMPTS

Address Your Wounds

What personal or world events are keeping you from seeing joy in your life right now?

What are you afraid will happen if you experience joy?

Channel Your Wisdom

Joy and delight are always there; sometimes they're just hidden. Describe joy.

What does it look like? Study it like an anthropologist.

Where does it reside?

Where is it in disguise?

What makes it come to life? Be specific.

Bliss List: In these dark moments, it often feels like you will never experience joy again, but even during difficult times, joy is right beneath your very nose. Let your Joyful Heart create a bliss list by writing about the joys in each space.

Example:

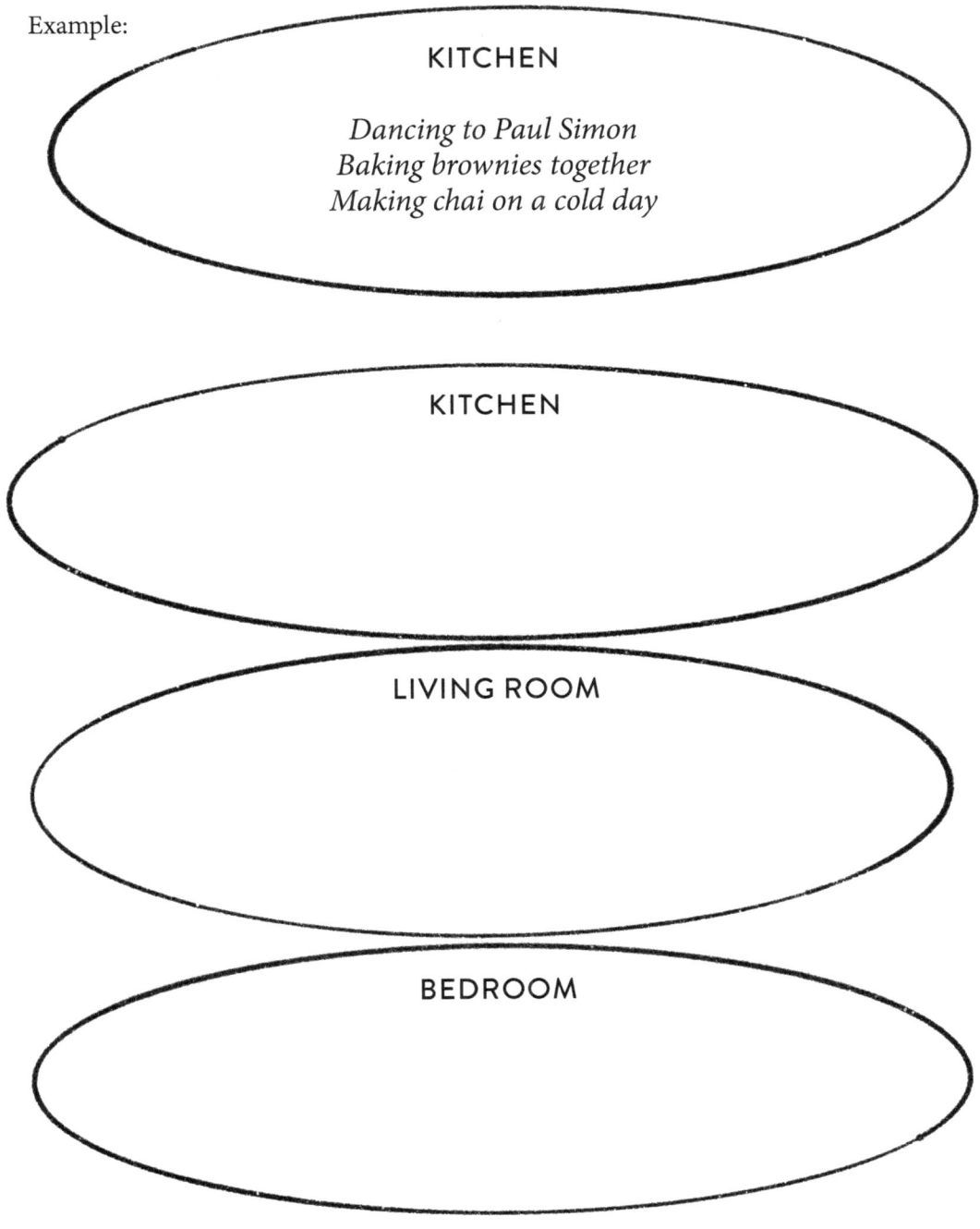

KITCHEN

Dancing to Paul Simon
Baking brownies together
Making chai on a cold day

KITCHEN

LIVING ROOM

BEDROOM

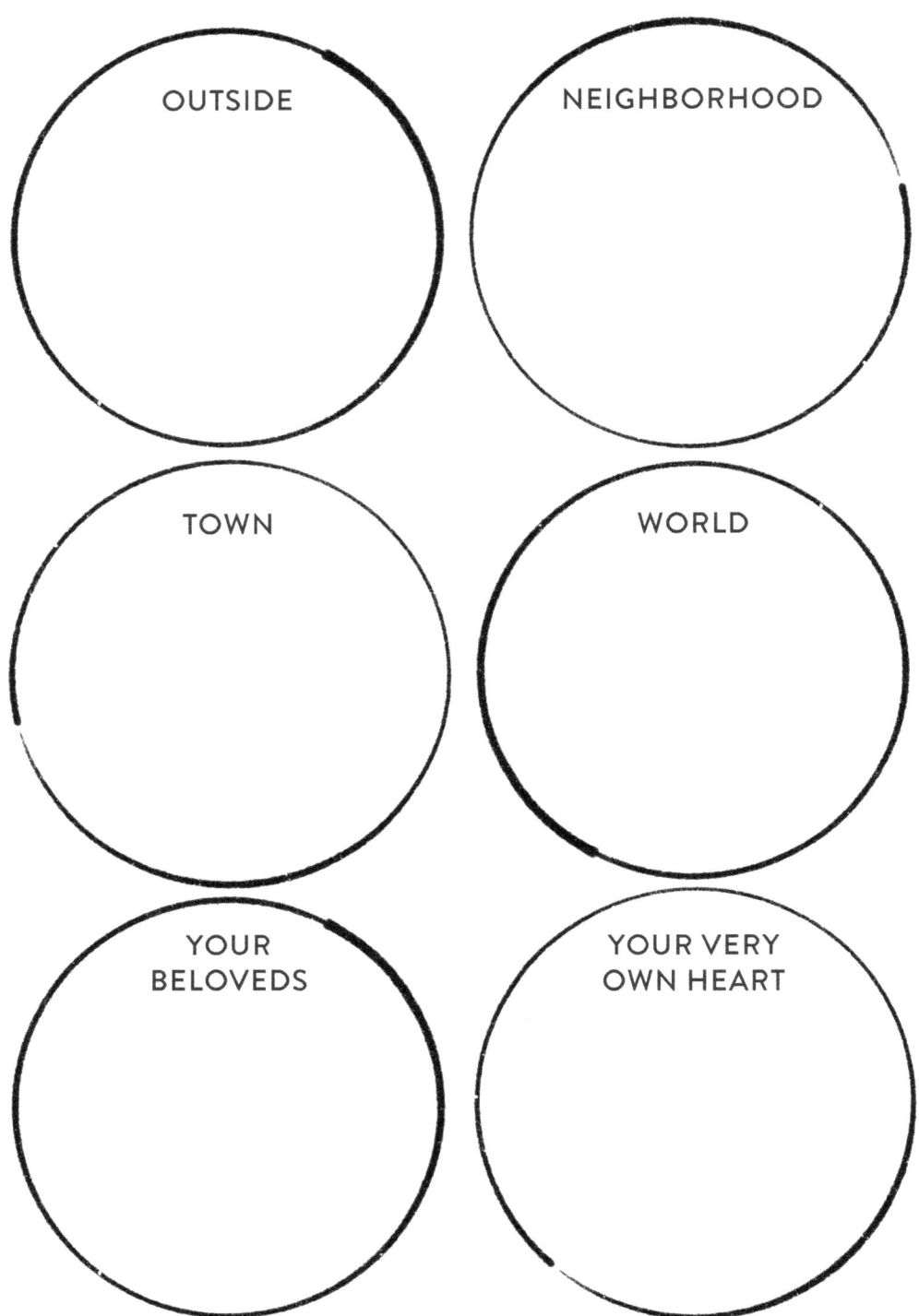

Bonus Activities: Create a Shrine of Blissful Objects somewhere where you can see it every day, or create a scavenger hunt for someone, hiding love notes or little gifts around the house.

CHAPTER 17
Puzzle Pieces

In November of 2020, Jamie, Geo, and I took a road trip from Illinois to North Carolina and rented a little beach house. We were exhausted from homeschooling Geo while remotely working our full-time jobs and being in a constant state of anxiety. We were also sad and terrified for my biological father, who had recently been diagnosed with cancer and was undergoing chemotherapy. We needed to regroup emotionally and hoped the beach would do the trick.

When we checked into the house, I discovered a shelf full of games and puzzles. Besides doing little ones with Geo, I had never really been a puzzle person. But the shelf held a 1,000-piecer, and I figured I might take a stab at it that night after we got a glimpse of the ocean.

Since the warmth and the sun were so different from the gray Midwest, North Carolina felt like an alternate universe. As soon as we stepped onto the sand, our minds and hearts expanded in relief. I watched Jamie watching the waves, and I saw a joy and awe I had not seen in quite some time on my husband's face. Geo unzipped his hoodie and rolled up the cuffs of his pants, splashing in the surf. I sat cross-legged in the sand, closed my eyes, and breathed in the salty air, feeling tears of release and gratitude build up in my eye creases. My god, did this feel good. After months of claustrophobic restriction, it felt freeing to be on a wide, expansive shoreline with the endless ocean before us.

When the sun began to set, we went for a walk along the water's edge. While Geo ran ahead, Jamie and I talked openly about the many transitions we were traversing. The pandemic and my father's cancer battle were putting things into perspective, making us reassess the lives we were living. Jamie knew he wanted to switch careers, I was burnt out by the university teaching grind, and we agreed that living in a cold place during lockdowns was making us question if we wanted to live in a northern climate long-term. Everything felt jumbled and uncertain, but what did feel certain was this: Being on Wrightsville Beach made our shoulders loosen from our ears and our smiles return to our faces.

The first night at the beach house, when dusk fell, we ate dinner with the front door open, and the ocean churned faintly in the distance, blowing a cool breeze through the screen. When Jamie and Geo retreated to the couch for crafts and movies, I started the 1,000-piece puzzle. It was a picture of different colored doors with frames of varying materials—stone, brick, and wood. When I dumped the pieces onto the table, it was overwhelming. How would I ever form this mess into a picture?

Instinctively, I separated the pieces into colored piles and made another mound for those with distinctive features like doorknockers and elaborate hinges. Hours passed as my sole focus remained fixated on the nuances of each piece. It felt nice to concentrate on something without distractions pulling my mind in a million directions. Even as the clock approached 11:00 p.m., it was hard to pull away.

The next afternoon, we walked the beach, talking about our current state of ambiguity. As we collected seashells and watched the sun set over the pier, we deliberated and dreamed. What did we want from this maddening, magnificent life? What did we want for our future? What did we want for Geo?

We didn't know the answers to those questions. All we could talk about was what we didn't want. I didn't want to teach back-to-back university classes with no lunch break. Jamie didn't want to be at the beck and call of a company that didn't value family time. We no longer wanted to suffer six-month winters and gray skies.

When we returned from our walk, we ate dinner with the door open again, and I got back to my puzzle. I began the slow process of seeing which pieces paired together and which belonged to other patches of the picture. I tried to force some, but when their little cutouts didn't quite fit, I surrendered and searched for the right ones. When the clock struck 11, I had completed small but satisfying portions of the puzzle.

The next day, we went for our usual sunset walk. As Geo chased the sandpipers that scurried along the seafoam, Jamie and I talked about the kind of life that might fit us better. Jobs we loved. Being our own bosses. Flexibility. Freedom. More attention paid to our marriage, to our son, to adventure. More time in sunnier places.

At the end of the walk, we had a little more clarity on which pieces belonged, but we had no idea how they would all fit together. That night, as Jamie prepared dinner in the cottage kitchen, I sat in a rocking chair on the porch and journaled. As I listened to the ocean, I reflected on how North Carolina had been calling to us for months. We hadn't known why, but we had decided to go, and I was so glad because this time of looking out at the wide open water was opening us up to new possibilities.

Over the course of the week, I connected one puzzle segment to the next, and eventually, they became an almost complete larger picture. We went for more beach walks and made more decisions: I wanted my side passion of coaching female authors to eventually become my full-time profession. It was the thing that brought me the most joy. We also wanted to fulfill a dream that had been on our bucket list for a decade: to travel the U.S. in a camper. We decided to stop putting it off and set a date for our maiden voyage the following summer. Both decisions would require great sacrifices, but the bigger picture was coming together.

On checkout day, I still had 50 or so pieces left—the ones with the finest details, hardest to discern. Sure. I would have loved to finish. But it felt immensely satisfying. All those little pieces had become something.

On a 70-degree day, during our final beach walk before heading back to Illinois, Jamie and I took one last look at the waves and decided that something was clear. We wanted to live life on our own terms. We wanted to stop all the busyness. We wanted to incorporate the tranquility of nature into our daily routines.

Our lives were a 1,000-piece puzzle, and here we were, adding the next segment to our incomplete but beautiful picture.

I could see it.

I could feel it.

It fit.

JOURNALING PROMPTS

Address Your Wounds

What is the treadmill you can't get off of or the frantic behaviors you're addicted to?

What is cluttering up your life or perspective?

Channel Your Wisdom

If this year or month was your last on this precious planet, how would you be spending your time?

In her book, *Untamed*, Glennon Doyle asks, "What's the truest most beautiful story about your life that you can imagine?" How would you answer that question?

Letter: Your life is a puzzle. Let your Clear Heart tell you what no longer fits and what new picture you're forming.

Date _____

Dear _____ ,

From my 10,000-foot view, I can clearly see the picture you want to form, but I know it seems that you're just swimming in the pieces. Here's the best way to get clear. Let's do away with what does NOT fit. What don't you want to spend the next year or decade doing? Put these things in your LESS or NO MORE list.

LESS:

_____
_____
_____
_____
_____

NO MORE:

_____
_____
_____
_____
_____

Now imagine your magnificent life, as if anything were possible. Describe in detail what that picture looks like. Where do you live, who are you with, what are you doing? Most importantly, how do you feel?

Here's a change you can make immediately toward that clearer picture:

If time were fleeting and urgent, what would you do differently in the next month or year?

_____

_____

_____

_____

It's time to make some changes, my love,
Your Clear Heart

P.S. Don't forget to read this back to yourself.

Bonus Activity: Draw a picture of the magnificent life you described above.

CHAPTER 18

The Last First Snowfall

It's the first snowstorm of the year. As dusk falls, so do the tiny snowflakes, and the twinkle lights in the neighborhood switch on, giving everything a magical glimmer. The frozen backyard collects a pristine layer of the fluffy stuff, enticing us as we eat our dinner and look out the window.

When Geo and I finish our plates, we hop up and wrap ourselves in layers to run outside, the snow crunching beneath our boots. Scooping up clumps, we pack them in our hands, forming lopsided snowballs. When we toss them at each other, flecks fall off like glitter in the glow of the twinkle lights that drape our yard. The air is fresh but cold in our noses and lungs as we run, pant, and laugh. We play tag and make snow angels until our cheeks flush and our bodies sweat under our coats.

Through the fogged windows, our warm house glows, and Jamie waves from the kitchen. Geo and I stand in the middle of the yard, looking out at the neighbors' homes, the sky. There's nothing and no one outside. Just us. The world is still and silent besides the sound of new flakes crackling as they join the sheet of snow on our deck. Geo is giddy, but I'm silently saying goodbye. This will be our last winter in Illinois.

We have reached our threshold of cold and grey skies. So I choose to look at this snowfall not with my usual annoyance of all things winter but as a generous send-off. I try to hold it in my heart with nostalgia. Geo heads to the back door, tapping his boots on the frame to rid them of snow, then pulling off his itchy hat and scarf. Still, I stay outside a minute longer, looking around at the Midwest landscape that has simultaneously given us so much hardship and also so much reprieve. We have a few more months here, and we don't know where we'll end up, but I nod my head to it: the last of the first snowfalls we'll ever witness here.

JOURNALING PROMPTS

Address Your Wounds

Any positive change or growth also comes with closure. What relationships and situations feel like they need closure or haven't gotten a proper goodbye?

What rituals or honoring ceremonies would help provide closure so that your soul can move on?[7]

---

[7] A good resource for this is Day Schildkret's book, *Hello, Goodbye*.

Channel Your Wisdom

If you were to write a letter to a person, place, or situation that needs closure, who would you write it to and why?

Letter: Write a letter to a person, place, or situation, giving it proper closure. You can choose whether you want to send the letter or not. If not, can you create a ritual around the letter? Tear it? Burn it? What feels like release?

Date _____

Dear _____,

You have been important in my life because:

_____

_____

_____

_____

_____

_____

_____

_____

But now I need to say goodbye because my heart needs:

_____

_____

_____

I want you to know that:

And what I want you to say to me is:

All my love,

CHAPTER 19
That's Not Your Yard

As the pandemic wore on and the dirty snow became icy mud, we were stuck in the muck too. Jamie was torn about his next professional steps and Geo missed his friends.

At first, I tried all of the things: the pep talks, the fixing. "Have you thought about… What if you…The silver lining is…"

I was "bright-siding"—putting the positive spin on the situation and not allowing the other person to feel their feelings or figure out creative solutions for themselves. Then, when they didn't cheer up right away, I retreated. The only thing that really helped was our walks.

Jamie, Geo, and I left our home at 3:30 every afternoon to walk the neighborhood. Wrapped in layers and scarves, we confronted the cold to get some fresh air and exercise. One day, as we walked past a neighbor's front yard, Geo noticed a golf ball on their snow-spotted grass.

"What's this doing here?" he asked. He swung his foot back to kick it. Jamie and I stopped him.

"Leave it alone," I said. "That's not your yard."

As soon as the words left my mouth, I repeated them to myself.

"Leave it alone. That's not your yard."

It is easy to distinguish one neighbor's property from the next. Some even have fences for extra delineation, but in terms of emotional turf, I'm always trying to tidy up other people's lawns, thinking it's my job to tend and mend. I see their grass growing tall, their weeds taking over, and I think it's my responsibility to clean it up. I come right over without an invitation, pushing a lawnmower. Somehow, I've designated myself the lawn maintenance manager of the entire universe.

I often forget that my job is to be their neighbor, not their gardener. My job, mostly, is to show that I'm right there on the other side of the fence, holding space and listening, but not fixing.

I know this because I have people in my life who are fixers, and as soon as they come over to my yard and start telling me what to do, it feels like an intrusion, like they don't trust me to figure it out. My immediate reaction is to escort them right out rather than let them in.

So, when Geo complained to me about his remote school lessons or a friend vented about her spouse, I resisted the urge to tell them my high-horse solutions. I'd mentally repeat, *That's not your yard,* and I'd just listen. I repeated Geo's emotions back to him. "That's so hard. You must be so upset." Rather than walking away to avoid his tantrums, I hugged him. It took all of my energy not to retreat or offer advice, but after enough hugging, he'd eventually say, "Well, I guess I'll go play with my Legos now," and that was that.

With Jamie, I did the same. Listen. Acknowledge. Hug.

It worked so well, I started doing it to myself in my journal, being a neighbor to my feelings, acknowledging them, not always needing to fix them.

"That's so hard," I said to myself over and over again.

That phrase became the top response to anything that I or anyone else was experiencing. The immediate reaction was a softening, a relief. *Yes, it IS so hard. Thank you for seeing that.*

But with someone who was gossiping all the time or a close friend who was making reckless choices, it was a bit more complicated. I acknowledged that they were going through a hard time, but I also knew that I could not allow their behavior around me or my family. It was one thing to hold space for their pain, it was another to repeatedly allow them to trample all over my yard.

So then came the next step—the installation of the fence. What would I allow in, and what would I not allow?

Gossip and lies? Not allowed in.

Someone who'd betrayed me and then pretended to be cordial? Not allowed in.

But joy? Peace? Love?

Allowed.

Allowed.

Allowed.

JOURNAL PROMPTS

Address Your Wounds

What other yards are you tending?

What freedom do you need to give the other person? What choices do they need to make on their own?

Channel Your Wisdom

Who would you be if you used your co-dependent energy to tend to your own yard instead?

List: In what ways can you be a listener rather than a fixer?

Rules: Who is trying to landscape your yard? Who is littering all over your yard? What fences (boundaries) do you need to put up? Make a list of rules for how people should interact with and respect you, your space, and your energy.

CHAPTER 20

The Opposite of Loss

On a sunny Saturday that April, I got the call that my father was losing his cancer battle and was not going to make it. The nurse said that when I visited him the next day, it would likely be the last time I saw him. It was a crisp spring morning, and Jamie and I had just dropped Geo off at his kid's science class.

We were sitting in a strip mall parking lot because I was about to purchase a gift for my sister. Unbeknownst to her, her boyfriend would propose to her that afternoon. And we were all going to meet up afterward to congratulate them. I wanted to find the perfect gift.

And then I got the news about my father.

My parents had divorced when I was young. My mom later married my stepdad and had my sister, but my father didn't remarry. So I shared many of my Sundays with him, just the two of us driving around or stopping at my Grandma Kenney's house for a visit. When I became an adult, my father and I went on family trips together to Ireland and Hawaii, strengthening our bond.

But one of his proudest experiences was becoming a grandfather to Geo, who called him *Dad-o* (a play on the Irish word for Grandpa). Then my father got the news that he had cancer. One short year later, he was leaving this world. When I hung up the phone, I sobbed in the passenger seat of our truck as Jamie rubbed my back. And when I was too overwhelmed to stay in the truck for one more minute, I asked Jamie to drive me to Home Depot.

Despite my grief, I instinctively felt that I wanted to get my sister and her partner something important, something meaningful, not some throwaway knickknack. I wanted to give them a tree. Bleary-eyed, I stumbled through the outdoor garden section, wondering how it was even possible to hold two opposing emotions in my heart at the same time, joy and elation for my sister, deep grief and mourning for my father, whose life was being cut short at age 57.

How do we carry on when such loss is at our doorstep?

As Jamie and I roamed the outdoor aisles of the garden center, I felt like a zombie. I was outside of my body, floating, untethered, in an alternate reality. Other people milled about, grabbing pansies for their garden, seemingly without a care in the world. I felt lost.

I never imagined that I would be fatherless at such a young age. As I walked around,

I saw a section that said "flowering trees," and something in my broken heart warmed a bit. I checked all the tags to see what kind of flowers they yielded until I found the perfect one. It would bloom every spring to remind my sister and her partner of the day they decided to spend their life together.

As we secured the tree in the bed of Jamie's truck, that little sapling planted a tiny bloom in my heart. Love would still flower, even amid loss.

We celebrated the wonderful engagement that evening. And then, the next morning, I said goodbye to my father.

Within a span of 24 hours, I had embraced my sister as she leapt into my arms after her proposal, and I had rubbed the thin, shaking hand of my father, who was leaving this world.

The contrasts of that spring were so shocking to me that I don't know how my heart did not split into two.

At my father's memorial service, I sobbed as soldiers played "Taps" and handed me his folded military flag. I jumped with each gun blast of the salute, feeling like I had been shot.

And also that spring, there were moments of love, of joy, of awe: of jumping on the trampoline with Geo, drinking a mint julep and wearing a silly hat at my sister's Kentucky Derby party.

How was it possible to hold love and loss in my heart at once?

My father's passing and a family health crisis have caused us all to be more cognizant of our mortality. And poor Geo has recently realized that our time on this earth is finite. One night, he called me into his room, asking what happens when we die. He was terrified, knowing that there would be a time when he would be here and Jamie and I would not. With my own tears in my throat, I tried to soothe him. But how could I console my son when these very same terrors keep me up at night?

I said that none of us knows what the afterlife will bring. So what if we imagined the most beautiful place where all spirits meet? I said that one way to lessen your worry is to recite a list of things you're grateful for. I said, "I'll guide you through a meditation and ease your pain." But as I rubbed his head and whispered soothing images of sunshine pouring into his heart, I wondered to myself, *How do we keep living in the wake of such loss?*

Knowing that loss is inevitable, how do we not let it consume us?

A flood of images came into my brain. One of when I was little: my father taking me to the bookstore (our favorite place) and to Taco Bell (his least favorite but my ultimate), and another memory of my father renting a red Mustang convertible on a family trip so we could ride along the beach with the wind in our hair.

I thought of the last words he ever said when he was in the hospital while on the phone with Geo. "How are you feeling, Dad-o?" Geo asked, and my father answered, "A whole lot better now that I'm talking to you." Cleaning out my father's house after his passing, I found the get-well cards that Geo had drawn for him. They completely covered the side of my father's refrigerator. His cupboards were full of mugs that had pictures of him and Geo on them. And the computer mouse pad he used every day was a family photo collage I had given him for Christmas.

And it hits me. I want to tell Geo that the opposite of death is not life. It is not merely existing. The opposite of loss is love.

It is loving your people. It is the memory of a father taking his daughter to a fast food place he hated because he knew she loved it. It is when I drink a mint julep and toast my sister's engagement, so delighted in her happiness. It is when I jump on the trampoline with Geo.

It is when Jamie cooks us dinner every night. It is when Geo gives Jamie and me family hugs. It is when I guide Geo through a meditation to ease his worries, and he falls asleep instantly.

The opposite of loss is not life. It is not merely the tree itself. It is the flowering blooms that fill your heart with joy and awe.

And so I whisper to Geo as he sleeps peacefully, "Love is not merely the opposite of loss, my dear. It is the answer to it."

JOURNALING PROMPTS

Address Your Wounds

What has loss looked like in your life?

What has it taught you?

Channel Your Wisdom

What has love looked like in your life?

What has it taught you?

Letter 1: Write a thank you letter *to* Love.

Date _____

Dear Love,

Thank you for these sweet moments:

_____

_____

_____

_____

_____

_____

And thank you for teaching me:

_____

_____

_____

_____

_____

I know that Love is always the answer,

_____

Letter 2: Write a letter to yourself *from* Love, as author Elizabeth Gilbert does every morning.

Date _____

Dear _____ ,

I want you to know that:

_____

_____

_____

_____

_____

I am amazed by you because:

_____

_____

_____

_____

_____

Here for you always,
Love

CHAPTER 21

You Are Welcome Here

A week after my father passed, I sat on the floor of my office in my sweatpants, weeping. As a balm for my soul, I grabbed my journal and penned this letter to myself. First, I offered it as a meditation on my podcast, *Heart of the Story*, but then I learned about the Internal Family Systems model for self-integration and healing trauma, which says that "our core self knows how to heal." I realized how my heart had intuitively been trying to welcome all of my hurting parts through this journaling exercise. Here is what I wrote.

* * *

If you are lonely or feel isolated in your suffering, you are welcome here.

If you feel like a shell of yourself, like your soul has been scooped out from within and now pulses outside your body, exposed and unprotected, you are welcome here.

If you are exhausted, so worn out from heartache, and yet restless, aimless, pacing, circling, you are welcome here.

If you are lost, floating, seemingly without direction, in the middle of a great abyss with no one to tell you where to go or which direction to head, you are welcome here.

If you feel anxious, so worn out by life and also like a child so deeply in need of nurturing, you are welcome here.

If you are mourning, mourning, mourning the loss of everything you thought would be forever, everything you thought you knew, you are welcome here.

Where is here, my love? Where is here?

Here is sitting on the floor in your tattered sweats with your unwashed hair and your puffy eyes.

Here is a mirror where you look into your own devastated face, and you see all that it has been through, and you say, Oh, Sweetheart, I'm sorry. Honey, come here. Let me hold you.

Here is the ground where you curl up in a ball and sob and rock yourself until the feeling has run its course. Here is the space in the room where the sun slants perfectly across your legs, reaches out to pat your knee, and says, There there, my dear. There there.

Here is the open window where the birds chirp and chatter, not because they are oblivious to your heartache but because they remind you of what you've always known: that you are not alone. You have never been alone. You are always, always welcome. Here.

JOURNALING PROMPTS

Address Your Wounds

In what ways do you feel restless, aimless, anxious, or unprotected?

What are the parts of you that are suffering?

How does this feel physically in your body?

Channel Your Wisdom

What messages do your hurting parts need to hear?

How would your hurting parts feel if they didn't have to carry those burdens anymore? What joyous activities would they be participating in?[8]

Imagine the most lovely, safe place that would be a refuge for your suffering parts. Describe it in detail.

---

8   Inspired by Internal Family Systems work: https://ifs-institute.com/ and Ann Baker: https://annpetrusbaker.com/

Letter: Now let's write a "You Are Welcome Here" letter for all of your parts.

Date _____

Dear _____ ,

When you feel young and vulnerable in these ways:

_____

_____

_____

because:

_____

_____

_____

_____ , you are welcome here.

When you feel controlling in these ways:

_____

_____

_____

_____

because:

_____

_____

_____

_____ , you are welcome here.

When you feel impulsive in these ways:

_____

_____

_____

_____

because:

_____

_____

_____

_____

_____ , you are welcome here.

Where is here, my love?

Here is:

_____

_____

_____

_____

_____

_____

_____

_____

_____

_____

You are always welcome here,
Your Whole Heart

P.S. Don't forget to read this back to yourself.

SECTION 4

Charting a New Course

CHAPTER 22

The Hum of Your Heart

In California, on retreat, I was paying attention to the things with wings—the hummingbirds, the monarchs, and later the powerful women in my retreat group whose souls were taking flight with every minute of self-care they soaked in. We colored, we danced, and we sang about a nation of women with wings. And it did feel like we were soaring with the freedom of not having to attend to the monotony of our lives, the screens, and lists.

I was so absorbed in my surroundings, deeply smelling the eucalyptus and sage, the wildflowers and pampas grass. I was feeling the textures—the spiky softness of the lush green lawn as I walked barefoot across it, the warm sulfuric water in the clawfoot hot springs tubs as the waves crashed into the rocks below, creating swirls of seafoam. I was watching the sun move across the sky each day, first creating a soft pink glow at the base of the bluffs and then coming up over the mountain and settling on my mug of golden milk in the morning. At mid-day, it blazed across the middle of the ocean as it warmed my balcony and the skin of the lizards who sunbathed on the wood railing. In the afternoon, it glowed over the garden as people read and rested in Adirondack chairs. Then, finally, it set while the seals barked and the frogs peeped. A hummingbird levitated over a flower, taking in all of it.

I was paying attention to these things because I was finally sitting in stillness. I'd been in constant motion and trauma for so long that I'd forgotten how impactful it was to go to another location, turn off technology, and rest. The retreat leader, Renée Trudeau, asked us to pause repeatedly, place our hands over our hearts, and check in with how we felt, what we needed, and what we wanted to do. The first time I sat in stillness and did this, I got teary-eyed. I'd been in such a reactive, hypervigilant mode from the pandemic and my father's passing that I hadn't stopped to ask myself what I actually wanted to do in a very long time.

I had come to the retreat to heal from grief and to chart a new course. As a family, we were headed into new territory, physically and emotionally, and I felt like my brain was buzzing with the logistics of packing and storage containers. Still, I had no idea what my own heart felt. In times of stress, experts say that we either over-function or under-function, and I am, without a doubt, a severe over-functioner. I over-function when something hard happens but also when I'm excited about the new road and adventures ahead. My anxiety tells me that the more I plan, the more control I'll have over positive outcomes. (Insert ironic laugh here.) But what always helps is LESS action—stopping, going on retreat, resting.

Resting to me doesn't only mean naps, though those always help. It means sitting and breathing. It means daydreaming. It means yoga nidra. It means looking out at nature. It means slow walking, slow eating, and slow journaling. It means doing 50 percent less of the things on my to-do list and doing the remaining things at a 50 percent slower pace than I would typically do them. The retreat leader said she goes on retreat every 90 days in order to check in and course correct, because you don't know how much all the chaos and technology are impacting you until you stop. That's when you go from seeing the world in black and white to technicolor.

It's not until you truly see grass and leaves again, until you smell the sweet scent of flowers, until you see wings aflutter, that you're reminded that life is going on elsewhere, that beauty is still to be found, and you realize that life may have covered your soul in a foot of mud, but inside your heart, there's a hummingbird that's been beating all along. With its emerald wings and magenta neck, it has been fluttering, completely unbeknownst to you, and sometimes it feels about 2,000 miles away. But it is not a plane ride away, my love; it's as close as the stroke of the pen on your page, telling you to neglect the buzz of your brain and to finally nurture the hum of your heart.

JOURNALING PROMPTS

Address Your Wounds

In times of good and bad stress, do you under-function or over-function?

What does that look like?

Channel Your Wisdom

What does REST look like to you?

Yoga nidra expert, Tracee Stanley, asks this question that I love: "Who would you be if you were truly rested?"⁹

---

9   Stanley, *Radiant Rest*

Check In: Sit in stillness for a few moments, with your hand on your heart, and answer these questions. The first three are from retreat leader, Renée Trudeau, who says that "self-care is about attuning and responding to your needs and desires moment to moment."[10]

Date _____

How do you feel?

_____

_____

_____

_____

_____

What do you need?

_____

_____

_____

_____

What do you want?

_____

_____

_____

---

10   Trudeau, "Ready to Prioritize Your Self-Care? Start Here."

Based on the previous three questions, what do you want to do right now or today or in the near future?

CHAPTER 23

Coyotes

Door County, Wisconsin, has become our favorite place to be in the summertime. We discovered it years ago and stayed for a weekend the first time, then a week the following summer, then 10 days the next. So we knew it would be the first stop on our summer road trip in our Airstream.

I was out for a jog the first morning in Door County when I first caught sight of something out of the corner of my eye. It had menacing teeth, a hunched back, and pouncing legs.

It was a coyote.

I jumped, my heart sprinting, my pulse in my ears. But none of this made sense. I was out on the lakefront path, near an ice cream shop and the Ephraim village hall.

What the heck was a coyote doing here? Just as I was about to run in the opposite direction, I noticed its unmoving eyes and the stakes holding it to the ground. It was fake.

After surveying the area and spotting another faux coyote further down the lake path, I surmised that the coyotes were meant to keep the geese from pooping all over the sidewalk. Yet, the flocks still waddled around, grazing on the grass and leaving little presents behind. They cherished this spot as much as I did—the beach, the shallow swimming area, the view of the bluffs, and the sunset. The geese weren't going anywhere. And they didn't so much as flinch when they sauntered past the coyote.

Every morning during our week in Door County after that first coyote sighting, I would get up with the sun to slip on my running shoes and jog along the water. Though I knew the coyotes were there and were fake, each time I sensed their hulking figures, I jumped back, adrenaline pulsing through my arteries, my heart pounding, and my brain searching for an escape to safety. Meanwhile, the geese waddled around, oblivious to the very predators meant to scare them. They knew this threat wasn't real, but I didn't.

Like many humans, I've had enough trauma in my life that many ordinary things are coyotes to me. Any road, setting, scenario, or person that reminds me of a past difficult time is a threat. I'll be going about my ordinary day, maybe even feeling joyous, when suddenly something sends my adrenaline a-spiking, my heart a-racing, my vision a-tunneling. Other people can just walk or ride by the thing without the faintest of concerns. But not me.

For a long time, I have disliked this part of myself. Why can't I just be like a "normal person" who doesn't view so many things as a threat?

While I've always been a sensitive soul, there's something about new and unfamiliar paths that makes me see coyotes everywhere. I love adventure and travel and taking leaps (like we're doing on our road trip), yet these are the very things that cause me anxiety. Over the years, I've tried a variety of solutions: various therapies, exercise, CBD. But something that has helped me greatly is embodiment work. Being *in* my body and being *with* my body. We are allies, not enemies.

Dr. Hillary McBride published a book called *The Wisdom of Your Body*, and she is so compassionate with herself. Having been through major car accidents, she sees her coyotes on the road, and when she faces them, she talks to her body like a beloved. She calls her body a "she," and she talks to it tenderly. She reminds us that our body is trying to tell us things when it panics, including the fact that maybe we're still sensitive because we haven't dealt with this fully yet. This trauma, whatever it is, is still scary or sad for us, and that's when we need to be the most compassionate to it.[11]

My deep healing work with Ann Baker via Zoom has been practicing safety, so I can calm my nervous system. Her familiar, warm smile and hazel-grey eyes instantly settle me, and she helps me recognize other safety cues, things that make me feel calm and supported: Jamie, Geo, my puppies, my meditation cushion, and a lovely path at my local park. I seek out these cues as touchstones. I meditate on them so that my body can practice feeling safe and so that safety can become a familiar feeling in my body.

I was jogging up the hill the morning after I saw one of the fake coyotes, and the strangest thing happened. I like to head up into the hills for a run among the trees, and it seems odd because, out of the two spots—the lakeside path in the center of town and the wooded trails with the hills where no people are—the latter might have seemed like the scarier place, but it's an area where I feel calm and peaceful. So I was jogging, feeling this sense of calm, when I ran into a deer.

The next morning, it happened again, and every morning for the entire week. The deer would walk out onto the road in the glistening early light when the dew was still evaporating and misting the air. I would see the majestic creature, and I would stop, wonder washing through me and settling my heart. I would pause whatever podcast I was listening to, take out my earbuds, and slowly approach it.

We would lock eyes, and I would talk to it in my sweetest voice so that it knew I had good intentions. I would say, "Hi, beautiful. It's alright. You're alright." It would stand there, broadside, fully exposed, its ears twitching with my footsteps. But it stayed. We would offer kindness and trust with our eyes, saying, "I'm okay. You're okay. We're okay."

I'd get to a spot and stop, knowing that the deer was comfortable with me there. And we would have our beautiful exchange until, inevitably, a car would come by, and

---

11 McBride, *The Wisdom of Your Body*

the deer would dash off. We would meet there every morning in the glistening light and have our few moments of calm and connection.

Oh, the feeling of peace and delight, the serotonin and the oxytocin—the antidote to my anxiety. That's the feeling I seek when I practice safety. And now I've been making a lot of decisions based on if something feels like a deer or a coyote.

Yes. Coyotes are inevitable, but if I have a choice about something that will calm my nervous system, I'm going to choose that. And sometimes the healing balm comes to me unexpectedly.

On our very last evening in Door County, another interesting thing happened. We were driving around at dusk in a beautiful untouched area of land in Ellison Bay when we came upon a field with at least 20 deer, young and old. They were frolicking, playing, and even when our tires crunched on the gravel road, they knew we meant no harm. And so they kept prancing, delighting in each other. Such peace and ease and joy coursing through them. One, in particular, caught my attention—a doe—and she turned her head toward me, meeting my eyes. Something passed between us that I took as an invitation.

It was as if she was saying with her gaze, *Yes, I know that sometimes there are things to fear in this world, but this is yours too, my dear. This is your birthright here on earth as a natural creature—to frolic and nap. To play and nuzzle. To love.*

This is yours too, my dear. This is yours too.

JOURNALING PROMPTS

Address Your Wounds

Create a list of your "fake coyotes."

How does your body feel when it experiences these fake coyotes and what are the fears being triggered?

Now, make a list of "real coyotes" or warranted fears.

Channel Your Wisdom

What loving messages are your anxieties asking you to pay attention to?

When you hear the phrase "this is yours too" what comes to mind? What pleasures are your birthright?

Letter: Allow your Calm Heart to nurture you. Can you thank your body for showing you that those wounds are still tender, which is why you are still reacting to them? How can you reassure your nervous system that it can return to a calm state?

Date _____

Dear _____ ,

I know that you've been through so much and your heart sometimes relives old pain. Thank you for showing me that the following wounds are still tender:

_____

_____

_____

_____

_____

Let's comfort those old wounds. Here's what they need to know and to hear:

_____

_____

_____

_____

_____

Your nervous system needs a reminder that safety, love, and support are also available. These are the things that calm and reassure your nervous system.[12]

Smells:

_____

Sights:

_____

Sounds:

_____

Tastes:

_____

People:

_____

Places:

_____

Experiences:

_____

Please remember that joy and love are your birthright,
Your Calm Heart

P.S. Don't forget to read this back to yourself.

---

[12] Inspired by Ann Baker of Essence Health: https://annpetrusbaker.com/

CHAPTER 24

Finding New Shells

As we traveled from the Midwest to the East Coast and the South in our Airstream that summer, I began to understand why musicians age a hundred years over the span of one concert tour. When you're on the road, you truly LIVE, in good ways and bad ways. You are so manic to soak up all the experiences of every place that you find yourself unable to rest. You feel both proud to be living spontaneously and yearn for stability. And you're also at the mercy of Mother Nature, who gives you breezy, sunny days or torrential downpours, depending on her mood.

But when we arrived in Acadia, to our delight, nature kept the storms at bay, *and* our campsite happened to be on the ocean. THE OCEAN.

We'd open our camper door each morning and walk 50 feet to the Atlantic. I usually paddleboarded while Jamie and Geo explored the beach at low tide. Each time the tide goes out, it leaves all the rocks exposed. And in these natural bowls of rocks, there are tide pools and little puddles of water where the most amazing creatures can be found. You name it, you'll find it. It's like a treasure hunt presenting all sorts of gems: starfish, snails, and hermit crabs.

The hermit crabs interested me the most because when Geo was little, I used to read him a book called *A House for Hermit Crab*. The premise was that as the hermit crab got bigger, it would outgrow its shell, and it would need to leave the shell behind to go out and look for a new one.

It was always a hard process because little barnacles and sea anemones would grow in and around him and become his friends, so when he left the shell behind, it was sad. Then he would explore and get a new shell, which initially felt a little weird. But over time, he found new friends that would attach to the shell, and he would find a whole new community.

We are very much like the hermit crab, always growing and in need of different shells. It doesn't mean that the things we outgrow are not amazing. They just don't fit anymore. So just as we might change clothing styles or have a new set of friends, we always morph. And if we try to keep fitting into a mold that no longer suits us, there's great strain and pain. All of us have moments in our life where we can sit back and reflect: *What have I outgrown? Have my surroundings, jobs, and friends been changing with me?*

Years ago, the author Elizabeth Gilbert was living in a big home with a garden and a wonderful office library built in the attic, a place that she had put so much love into.

And one day she "looked around at that gorgeous home and realized: 'This is somebody else's dream.'"[13] And she sold it. It didn't mean that the house was bad. It just meant that it no longer fit her. And now it was time for somebody else to live in that shell. It was someone else's dream.

As we'd been moving from campsite to campsite all summer, I'd been in the midst of my biggest identity-shedding journey. Every role I had previously held was shifting. There had been so much change in our lives: My father had passed away, we'd sold our home and many of our things, I'd left university teaching to go full time with my writing coaching business, we'd gone on the road, and we had no idea where we'd live in the future. I also missed my mom and sister deeply. All the uncertainty could seem like a low tide.

But one morning, while watching Geo playing in the tide pools, I realized that this treasure trove only presents itself at low tide. That's when we're able to find all the treasures. At low tide.

And there had been so many treasures already. We'd sat around campfires, playing music and roasting marshmallows. Geo had made friends at campgrounds and had ridden bikes to get candy from the store. We'd swum in lakes and oceans and witnessed the wonders of Niagara Falls. Jamie got to show Geo Lake Winnipesaukee, where he'd spent his summers as a kid. We'd gotten down to the basics and realized we really didn't miss our material possessions.

And we'd gotten to see friends and family we hadn't seen in some time—our Michigan friends Julie and Dave, our Massachusetts friends Kelly and Mikey, Billy and Cheryl, Greg and Christina, Jenn and Rick. I met people in person whom I'd only ever known via Zoom, like my podcast producer Michelle, who lived in Maine. She and her musically talented husband Phil hosted us for an afternoon, and we had an impromptu jam session where Geo rocked out so hard he looked like an 80s metalhead. They sent us home with blueberry pie and a guitar pick, which Geo put in his special safe, that's how much of an impression the afternoon had on him.

But one of the treasures I also discovered was self-admiration.

I felt brave. I felt courageous. I felt proud of myself that I was willing to admit when something didn't fit. I was willing to take leaps and try out something new. It didn't mean there weren't days when I said to myself, *What the heck are you doing?* I still had self-doubt, just like every human being. But I kept following that instinctive voice inside of me that said, *It's time to try something different. Let's just see what's out there.*

You see, the hard times are when we develop the most trust in ourselves, when we look at the wreckage and say, *I'm still standing. I believe in myself. I hate uncertainty, but I'm willing to try new paths.* Low tide is when we see the treasures that have been within us all along.

We just have to be curious enough to go looking.

---

13   Gilbert, "Thought of the Day: Don't Live Somebody Else's Dream."

JOURNALING PROMPTS

Address Your Wounds

What shells have you shed in the past?

In what ways did they no longer fit?

Channel Your Wisdom

Who did you become as a result of your shedding?

What do you admire most about yourself as a result of having been through low tide moments and shell shedding?

Draw: First, draw your current shell. What feels right? What are you outgrowing? What feels confining or like someone else's dream?

Now, draw the shell that would suit you better for home life, work, relationships, and self-care. What feels expansive, free, and allows room for growth?

CHAPTER 25

Just Stand Up

Years ago, my Grandma Kenney went to an indoor water park with my cousins, who were little kids at the time. Despite my grandma's fear of water, my cousins convinced her to float in the lazy river with them. She was meandering along in the inner tube when she went to adjust herself and flipped over. Chaos ensued. She panicked and splashed, grasping for anything and anyone that would save her. She was drowning; she was sure of it. She flailed her arms, and when she would occasionally get air, she would scream and scream for help. My cousins, who'd been floating beside her yelled, "Just stand up, Grandma. Just stand up."

The water was only two and a half feet deep.

* * *

The water you're in is never as deep as you think it is, but you can only know this with perspective by standing up and realizing just how shallow it is.

After our road trip, everything was an unknown. Despite visiting many places, we hadn't found one that felt like the best warm-weather locale to settle down in. We had to figure out where we were going to live, what we were going to do for work, and where Geo was going to school. It didn't feel that much different from when we had moved to Chicago the decade prior, and I sat at the coffee shop paralyzed with uncertainty.

Just when I felt like I might drown in the chaos, I remembered my Grandma Kenney's lazy river story.

"Just stand up," I repeated to myself. "Just stand up."

Oh how I had a history of unnecessarily complicating everything and thinking things were worse than they actually were. So I read every helpful book I could get my hands on, like *Let It Be Easy* by Susie Moore, and *I Guess I Haven't Learned That Yet* by Shauna Niequist, and *Hope Anyway* by Leanna Tankersely. All of these women were writing about how to forge ahead in the midst of uncertainty, and their messages all boiled down to the same thing: Acknowledge where you are, give yourself grace, have trust in the unfolding, and let things be as easy as possible. Be a conduit rather than a controller. Be open to gifts and hints and possibilities.

Just stand up.

So slowly, this is what we did. First, I tried to float on life's inner tube as much as possible, paying attention to where it might be trying to take me. A friend told us about a beach town in Florida we might like, and we checked it out. Then we went back, and we wanted to keep going back. Jamie realized he could do private chef work for the vacationers and locals there, so he built a website and started making contacts. I realized I could lead women's writing and wellness retreats there. There was a good school nearby for Geo. We knew nothing would be perfect, and there were *many* obstacles: inflation, the crazy real estate boom, the rarity of finding a long-term rental in the area.

Each time it seemed like nothing would ever work out and the swells would pull me under, I stood up and got back on the inner tube—letting life guide me, trying to let things be easy for a bit, trying to trust that something would be around the corner. I saw a furnished long-term rental pop up on Zillow. It would get us through most of the school year while we tried out the area to see if we wanted to continue living in it. I knew that many other families would be vying for the house, it being a block from the beach—but an eerie calm came over me when I messaged the owner. He had so many applications that he decided to meet with prospective renters on Zoom. For whatever reason, he took a liking to us. We signed a lease.

As we packed a little trailer with our necessities and prepped for the 16-hour drive to Florida, I tried to think of myself riding the current of life, seeing where it would take me, and knowing that if I fell off my inner tube, I could always, simply, just stand up.

JOURNALING PROMPTS

Address Your Wounds

What water feels deep to you right now?

What are you making harder than it needs to be?

Channel Your Wisdom

How can you add ease and simplicity to your life?

In which areas can you trust life to show you the next steps?

The Life River: Think of this river as your present and future. You are starting to float ahead. Within the river, write a list of hints or directions from the universe that you've been receiving about where to go, what to do, who to get in contact with.

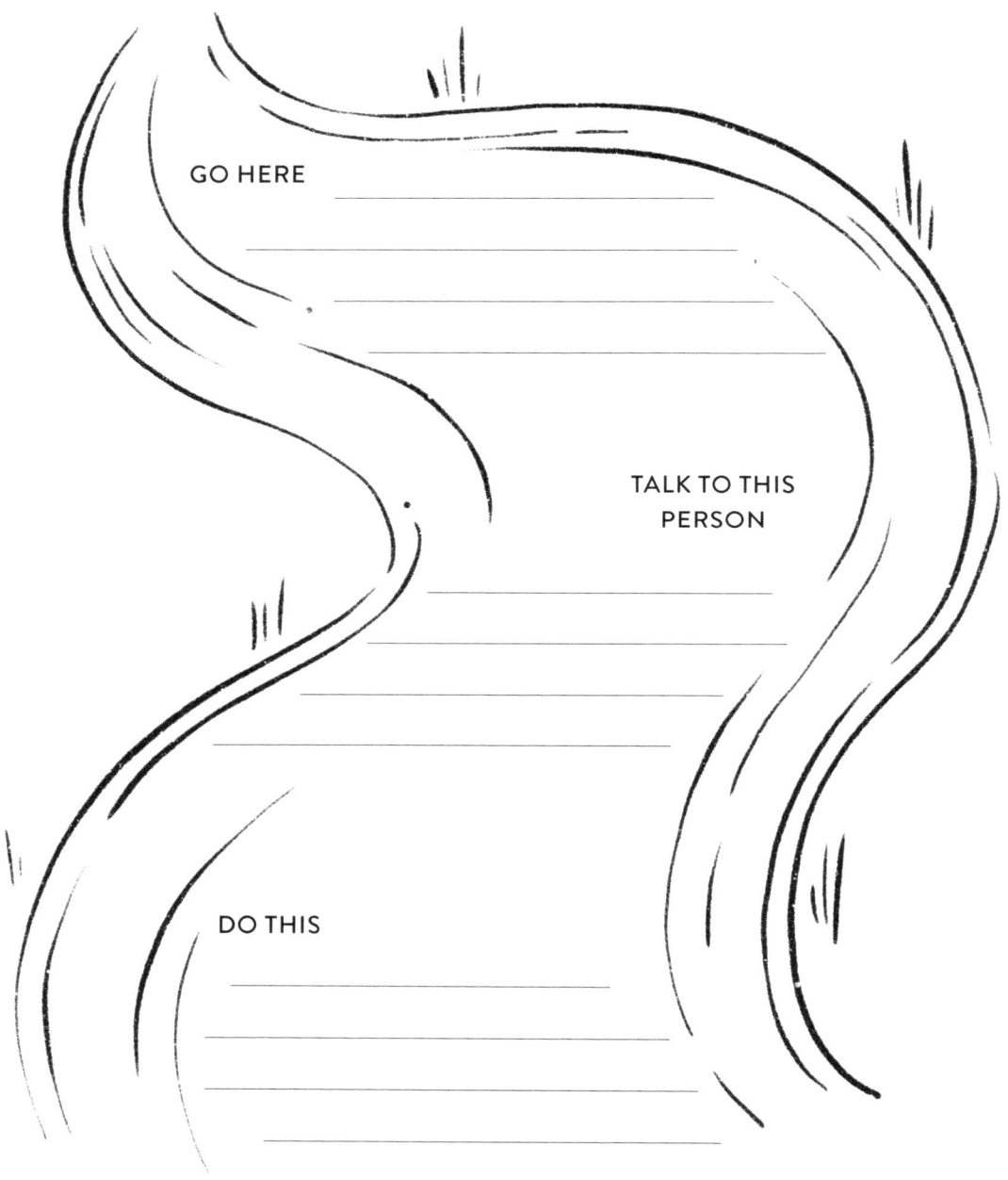

GO HERE

TALK TO THIS PERSON

DO THIS

CHAPTER 26

Walks in the Woods

The first time Jamie and I ever went for a hike in the woods I brought—I kid you not—suede fashion boots with a three-inch wedge heel.

I grew up wearing a hodge-podge of mismatched hand-me-downs—a pink hat, a purple scarf, an oversized coat. Our family was resourceful. If we outgrew our boots, we put plastic shopping bags over our socked-feet and stuffed them into gym shoes; that way, if we stepped in snow, the plastic would act as a water barrier. When I was in graduate school and had to pay for my own clothes with my own money, I spent it on trendy items—pointy-toed boots, coats that were flashy but non-insulated. After all, I was a city thing at that point, walking along Michigan Avenue every day to the Tribune Tower for my internship at *Chicago* magazine.

Though I'd always been an athletic person, I'd rarely hiked in the woods. There were no woods in Chicago. I was more likely to jog on the Lake Shore path, looking at the skyline. Then I met Jamie while we were both on vacation in Tampa, Florida, and we dated long distance between the East Coast and Midwest. During one of my early visits to see Jamie at his parents' lakehouse in Maine, I brought—god help me—my suede wedge boots.

On our first morning, when we prepped for a hike up the steep wooded hill that I'd have called a mountain in the Midwest, Jamie asked me where my winter boots were. I pointed to the wedges.

"No," he said. "Your hiking boots." Again, I pointed to the wedges, at which point he drove me straight to Eastern Mountain Sports and bought me a pair of Sorels.

In the woods, we were stripped bare. It was just us, the crack of the twigs, the creaking of birch limbs, the smell of the decaying leaves, the fog of our breaths, the glitter of the cold sun peeking through the branches. There was nothing to distract us.

Jamie moved thorny twigs to the side and pointed out roots on the trail so I wouldn't trip, even though I almost always did. He put his finger to his lips to signal silence so we could listen to a chickadee. I held his hand, swung it in the air, gave him spontaneous hugs, did dances, and ran around as he laughed at my energy. I pushed him to go further, steeper, to reap the reward of the hilltop view overlooking the lakes and the hills. He got me to slow down and observe.

Those walks and talks built our relationship and reminded us of what was most important. We were present with each other. We explored. We noticed the world. We were grateful for the simple things—the sight of a bright red cardinal or a timid doe. We were grateful for each other.

* * *

We've been together for 17 years now, and whenever our relationship feels hard, it's actually because life is hard and we deal with things differently. It reminds me of our New England hikes. The inclines are steep, and the terrain is tough, but we are here to help each other, not blame each other for the difficulty of the hike. Yet, when life gets difficult, that's what all of us are inclined to do—get mad at our partners for life's obstacles and our individual voids.

In the past, I've wanted Jamie to be my "everything" person—my running partner and my couch cuddling companion, my insightful introvert and my social extrovert, my practical planner and my spontaneous leaper. Basically, I've wanted Jamie to be a hybrid mix of him and me. While I never expect my sister or any of my friends to have multiple personalities, I've sometimes expected Jamie to because he's my spouse. And there have been times that Jamie wished I were more like him. He has gotten annoyed when my restless energy was too high, when I overbooked our weekend with too many plans, and when I left a mess in the kitchen. Wouldn't life be so much easier if we were more like each other?

But we can't forget our lessons from all of those walks in the woods—that our differences can be an asset. Our relationship excels, as it did on those trails, with the pull and the tug—me challenging Jamie to be a bit more adventurous, him encouraging me to slow down a little more. Otherwise, I would continue to race through life in the wrong boots, getting blisters and not noticing a single plant, and Jamie might get so wrapped up in the observing that he might not expand his vision to other summits. Those hikes had pushed us to grow—to still maintain our core selves but be flexible enough to try the other person's way too. We've had to do the same in our marriage. We've had to take all that energy we were using to bristle against our differences and channel it into gratitude. But we can't do anything if we aren't first paying attention to each other.

And so we go for walks when Geo's in school or at art class. As we walk, we're able to hold hands and talk without being interrupted. Anyone with kids can understand the strange freedom of strolling without a stroller, of walking for pleasure and not to a playground. It is peaceful and quiet. And when our hands clasp together, sometimes it's like a spark is shooting between us. We're connecting in that stripped-down way, like we're naked with each other, silent and synchronized, power passing between our palms.

I look at Jamie's handsome crinkly eyes, his peppered beard, the slant of his smile, and I feel overcome with love. Those eyes have watched me walk down the aisle and be rushed into the ER when I was near death. And his beard? He grew it when he found out I was pregnant after two unsuccessful years of IVF. The beard was a sort of good luck charm, growing as Geo grew in utero, and he's kept it ever since. Jamie's crooked smile lured me in on the first night I met him when we were having fun at a Florida bar, and now here it is still, 17 years later, despite so many moves and losses, and a global pandemic. Life has been hard, yes, but I love Jamie because he has traversed it with me. We have a deep history. Now, somehow, we're back in Florida, living in a beach town a few hours northwest of where we first met, trying it out for the school year. It's been a long, winding, oddly circular journey.

These days we go for sunset walks on the beach. At times, Jamie's pace quickens to match mine, and other times, I pause to notice a sandpiper or crab he points out. We talk about our marriage and Geo along the way—how we've stayed strong amid hardship, how we're raising a boy who's incredibly kind.

After one such walk, we stood in the surf for a moment, reflecting. The pink sky glowed all around us, and the pelicans soared overhead.

Jamie lifted my hand, then kissed the back of it.

"Well, Nader," he said, smiling. "I'd say that we've done a pretty darn good job so far."

"We certainly have," I said. "We certainly, certainly have."

Though we were at sea level, it felt like we were on a summit, looking down at all our hard work, at the beauty and challenges we've witnessed along the way, and relishing in it all.

Together.

JOURNALING PROMPTS

Address Your Wounds

What are the mountains you've climbed? Who have you climbed them with?

In what ways have you wanted the other person to be more like you?

In what ways have they wanted you to be more like them?

Channel Your Wisdom

In what ways have you morphed and been influenced positively by others?

In what ways have you positively influenced other people?

What goodness has resulted from collaborating with others?

Milestones: Reflect on your proudest moments and who helped you along the way. Write a list.

Date _____

What are the life milestones you most cherish? Celebrate them here by listing them.

_____

_____

_____

_____

_____

_____

You did so much to make these milestones happen. What are you proud of yourself for?

_____

_____

_____

_____

_____

_____

_____

Write down a list of people who helped you achieve these milestones.

_____

_____

_____

_____

_____

_____

_____

_____

We never walk this journey alone. Who can help you achieve future milestones?

_____

_____

_____

_____

_____

_____

_____

_____

CHAPTER 27

If You Want to Know Who I Am

As soon as Geo gets out of school each June, we now head straight to Door County, Wisconsin, and try to stay for as many weeks as possible before the school calendar calls us back. I was leading a women's writing retreat there and just felt so in love with the place that it made me fall more in love with myself. I realized, as I went for noticing walks each day, that as I was watching the universe in wonderment, it was watching me back with the same awe. I felt seen and known by creation, by nature, by my very own heart. What a gift it is to know yourself and to love her. So I wrote a piece about what it's like to see myself truly, and here is what I said.

If you want to know who I am, start your day with the dawn and get outside to see the sun coming up over the water. Move your body in any way that makes you feel the detoxifying wonders of sweat on your skin. Roll out a worn yoga mat and feel your muscles stretch with graceful movements. For breakfast, eat over-easy eggs and have mocha on the porch with your partner. Then sit in a nest chair and meditate to the sound of birdsong.

If you want to know who I am, carry a journal and pen with you everywhere. Write your heart out. Do work you love and help other women develop and publish their stories. Visit a bookstore or a library in the afternoon, then sit at a coffee shop for hours, lost in a good memoir.

If you want to know who I am, be part tomboy and part flower child. Some days you want to throw on running gear and a baseball hat. Other days, you want to adorn yourself with dangly turquoise earrings, a colorful tank top, and a flowy skirt. Feel beautiful and comfortable either way.

If you want to know who I am, walk. A lot. Walk the neighborhood to take a break during a work day, walk to alleviate anxiety, walk to see the moon coming up. Be whimsical and adventurous. Dance on the beach, play tag at the park, bounce on a trampoline, go down a waterslide, ride a go-kart.

If you want to know who I am, travel solo on retreat or with the people you love. Paddleboard the lake harbors of Wisconsin and the emerald gulf of Florida. Hike the volcanic mountains in San Marcos, Guatemala, and the Canadian Rockies in Banff. Eat cherry pie and go for a kayak ride in Glen Arbor, Michigan. Stop in any lake or ocean town, and enjoy pure summertime—beach strolls and book reading, water gun fights and wave-bobbing. At dusk, walk to Pearl in Ephraim and sit at a picnic table, laughing with friends as the crickets chirp and the sun sets.

As for food, if you want to know who I am, go to the best taco place in town, order chips, guac, and a taco-trio because anything with lime, avocado, and cilantro makes your heart sing. Or eat any of the thousands of delicious meals your chef husband has cooked for you—breakfast tostadas, honey goat cheese Brussels sprouts, rosemary and thyme potatoes, perfectly seared salmon.

If you want to know who I am, marvel at nature—the massive redwoods of California, the brown-eyed susans of the Midwest, and the tidepools of Maine. Be in awe of animals—cuddly puppies, fuzzy goslings, red-winged blackbirds, graceful dolphins.

If you want to know who I am, love your people. Go on girls' trips with your mom and sister or swim in your mom's backyard pool and swap sarcastic banter. Give your husband a million hugs and write him love notes. Take your son out for mother-son dates, just the two of you talking about anything he wants—robots, inventions, comic books, Legos. Give him all of your attention and treat him like the magnificent creature he is.

Most of all, see yourself as a magnificent creature, too. You are one and the same with the waters, the redwoods, the brown-eyed susans, with the mountains, the beaches, and the goslings. You are the love you give to others. You are the love they give to you. In your heart of hearts, you ARE love. And each new revelation makes you fall deeper and deeper in love with yourself.

LET'S TAKE A TOUR OF YOUR HEART

Tour: Be our guide and take us through the places, people, things, feelings, and experiences that make you YOU. Write an "If You Want to Know Who I Am" manifesto.

Date _____

Welcome to my heart. Let me show you around.

If you want to know who I am, visit:

_____

If you want to know who I am, watch:

_____

If you want to know who I am, eat and drink:

_____

If you want to know who I am, experience:

_____

If you want to know who I am, adorn yourself with:

_____

If you want to know who I am, create:

_____

If you want to know who I am, witness how I show love in these ways:

_____

Thank you for truly knowing me,

_____

CHAPTER 28

Forever Home

A few years ago, after my memoir was published and I was starting to think about my next writing project, the words "Home Is in Your Soul" came to me one day. I was sitting in the lakefront yard of the house we'd just purchased in northern Illinois. When we'd scoured the Chicago suburbs with our realtor, we'd said we were looking for our "forever home." And this certainly fit the bill: a light-filled house on a lake, the perfect place for raising Geo. At the very least, we'd stay there until he went off to college.

During our first year in our lovely lake home, we were in a very grounded place—Jamie and I had jobs in Chicago, Geo went to the neighborhood school, and my family was only 50 minutes away. So when the words "Home Is in Your Soul" came into my head, I thought, *How sweet of a notion. That will be my next book.* I had no idea it was a sort of life assignment I was about to embark on, not a book title.

Life basically said, *I know you think this place, this job, this dynamic, these friends, and this house you just took out a mortgage on will be your permanent home. But, Sweetie, I've got some hard news for you. It all changes, all the time.*

How much I've resisted this lesson. How desperately I've wanted to grasp onto something solid and permanent for my happiness. But life keeps coming back to re-teach me. In fact, as I write these words, I'm reminded that the house we bought in Illinois was not the first "forever home" we'd ever purchased.

Our first was our old house in rural Massachusetts. We bought it on the cusp of my 27th birthday, just before exchanging vows under a forsythia arbor. It was a two-story home with room for a family and a huge yard for a garden. I was neither a mother nor a green thumb yet, so I felt very grown up, thinking ahead like that. Still, I remember the realtor saying that when—not *if* but *when*—we wanted to resell it, we might have a hard time since it only had one bathroom. He said the average family lives in a house for five years.

Sell it? We were never leaving this charming home with its wood beams and potbelly stove. We were never leaving this idyllic town of rolling hills and forest preserves. He shrugged as if to say, *Things happen*, hinting at job changes, marital tension, financial gain or hardship. He was in his late 60s, a kind man who had lost his wife to cancer. He was selling the home where they'd raised their kids, and he was about to remarry. The look in his tender eyes said, *Anything can happen, just wait and see.*

I didn't want to believe him. In my late 20s, I lived in a world of plans and predictability. I thought that enough control could protect us from the worst. But then infertility and a near-death experience made me feel a bit shocked at how brutal life could be. Yet when we got pregnant naturally just before my 29th birthday (even though the doctors said it was impossible), I hoped and believed that the worst was behind us. I chuckle now at the thought. I look tenderly at that young-me, the same way the realtor did, not with pity but with a sort of sigh that says, *Oh, Honey, you have no idea.*

If I could talk to my younger self with absolute honesty, I'd say: Forget about the planning. Release your certainties. You have no idea that the worst is yet to come. And so is the best.

You have no idea that pregnancy will be absolutely awful. You will be so sick for months on end that you will truly feel like you are dying. And then the fog will lift at four months and you will feel glowy and beautiful and be elated at the miracle of feeling the baby kick. Then you will learn he has a kidney condition and he might not make it, and you will fall into the depths of despair. Yet somehow he will survive, and the birth will be part beautiful warrior labor and part hellish emergency C-section.

You have no idea that your sweet boy will make you feel the most smitten you've ever felt, how he'll nurse like a champ and also try to latch onto anything that looks like a nipple, including your husband's nose, which will have you both laughing for hours. You can't possibly fathom that you'll suffer from severe postpartum anxiety—*Is he breathing? Are the bottles clean? Does he have a fever?*—the relentless ongoing worry that leaves you sleep deprived. But there will also be moments of bliss—reading board books in the glider, teaching him to crawl, showing him the world, hearing that miraculous word "Mama" for the first time.

You have no idea that you'll watch your partner in awe, what a gentle father your broad-shouldered husband will be, tenderly changing and dressing your boy and letting him lay on his chest like a warm loaf of bread. But also, the two of you will have very different parenting styles—you'll hover unnecessarily, while your husband will be too lax sometimes. It's hard to imagine how difficult it will be to parent and partner—you'll realize you can't be Wife while you are Mama. You can't be carefree and funny and relaxed when you are bouncing and breastfeeding and burping.

You have no idea that your precious Massachusetts home will feel isolated and lonely in the winter months, that you'll suggest Illinois to be near your mom and sister, and that your nature-loving, homebody of a husband will say words that shock you: "You came to Massachusetts for me, I'll go to Chicago for you. You deserve that."

You have no idea that you will suffer many losses among family members and friends. People you thought were immortal and others you assumed would stick by you forever (there's that problematic word again) will disappear. And yet, miracles will befall you—angels will come out of the woodwork, surprising you with their generosity and deep love.

You have no idea that the profession you went to grad school for and worked so hard at—to be a professor—will lead to complete burnout, that waking up at 4:45 a.m. and working all day in a state of frantic panic is not sustainable. This may surprise you, but one day you will willingly give it up in pursuit of less hustle, less exhaustion, more heart-work, more helping women writers, more flexibility to be with your family. And believe it or not, you'll eventually say "no" more. You'll sit in stillness, go for slow walks to look at nature, and eat with awareness, savoring every bite. You'll play Legos with your son without worrying that you're behind on emails. You'll be able to sit, fully present, and listen to your husband without thinking about a lesson plan.

You have no idea that marriage will look like disagreements about TV volumes and thermostat temps and eating each other's dessert stashes, and it will also look like being at your husband's side when he is rushed to the ER after passing out in the kitchen. You will whisper desperate pleas to the universe to let him live because he makes everywhere home with his cooking and his hearty laugh. In a gift of great fortune, your wish will be granted and he will walk out of that hospital four days later, weak but alive, and it will make you look at every interaction thereafter with boundless gratitude.

You have no idea how achingly hard it will be to watch your son grow up so fast, how precious those times at the playground and library will become, how one day you won't be able to pick him up because he's almost your height, but he'll still snuggle with you on the couch. Oh how you'll love watching him draw and read and create and build and play. You don't know this yet, but of the many things he'll inherit from you, brutal honesty is at the top. He'll make fun of the loose skin that hangs from your arms. "You little stinker," you'll say, laughing, as he tugs on your wrinkly elbows. He will be your best teacher and your greatest gift.

You have no idea how much you will change with age—you'll morph from an anxious overachiever and people-pleaser to someone with clear boundaries who follows how she feels, yet you'll always be a work in progress. You will accumulate laugh lines and saggy eyelids, but you will love your strong body and your abundant heart for all it has gotten you through. You have no idea that this life—all of its trials and treasures—will ultimately make you cherish yourself.

Oh, young soul, I know you're standing in that Massachusetts "forever home," thinking you've got it all planned out, but you have no idea that you'll become an accidental wanderer—living in a city apartment, a suburban rental, a lake home in Northern Illinois. You don't know yet about the pandemic, the brutal winters in lockdown, the selling of your Illinois home and the purchase of your Airstream, living on the road in a 27-foot camper, the search for another place to plant your feet, ending up in Florida. For now, anyway.

I know it's hard to believe, but of all the things you will go searching for, home will feel the most elusive. But, Sweetheart, dear tender soul, here's what I want to tell you: You can go searching for miles and a lifetime, but the only forever home you're ever going to find is in your own soul. It is here for you any time of day or night, and even if you drift away from it, it will never drift away from you.

You can always, and forever, come back home to your heart.

Reflection: What have you spent a lifetime searching for that the outside world can never give you? What has been here all along in your own heart?

Date _____

Epilogue

Dear reader,

I was at my home office in Florida at the end of 2022, perched at my standing desk and answering emails, when Lucy's message popped up. She is the book's designer, and I knew her email would contain mockups of cover options. My pulse quickened as I opened the attachments. Would the cover capture the decade of spiritual lessons and years of essay writing that went into this manuscript? Would the design speak to women's hearts as deeply as I hoped it would?

I'd told Lucy that I wanted soft pinks and some kind of illustrated drawing, but the rest was up to her. I had to trust that she would understand my vision. When I opened the document and scrolled down to the third image—an illustration of a woman with a head made of flowers—my entire body tingled. *Yes*, my heart said. I never could have pictured it, but the flower woman was perfect. *Yes*. A full-bodied *yes*.

I answered Lucy's email, asking about colors and fonts, but the flower woman had to be the star of the show. *One more request,* I asked. In the version that Lucy had sent, the woman's right arm was covering her upper body. So I asked if we could switch arms, open up her heart-space, and if the bouquet's roots could extend down to her chest, forming her actual heart.

When Lucy sent me back the design that now graces the cover of the very book you're holding, my heart expanded like shoots coming up from soil. Literally. I felt it fully open up. This cover was one of seven possibilities, and each time I scrolled past it, my heart said, *Yes*. The flower woman was the most magnificent woman I'd ever seen, not because of any outward aesthetics, but because she lived from her heart—the source of her infinite wisdom.

Just for fun, I printed out the mock-designs and taped each one over a published book to see the seven different options spread out on our dining room table like real books. Jamie came over and picked up the copy that contained my beloved cover. "This one immediately caught my eye," he said. Geo pointed to the heart and added, "I love how it's made out of roots."

What was so captivating about the design? Was it because it showcased how your heart is the root of everything—the source of your presence and power, the gauge that gives you immediate feedback about how you truly feel, the purest representation of your spirit, unclouded by perfection or conformity?

Was it because it represents how the roots grow in the dark soil of your life, giving nutrients to the blooms that open in the light?

Yes to all of these things. But if you're wondering why the flower woman is so deeply captivating, it's because she, my dear reader, is YOU. YOU are the woman who lives from her heart. YOU are the woman with infinite wisdom.

May you see yourself in her and may you live a life of full-bodied YESes.

From my heart to yours,
Nadine

Resources

Many of these pieces were performed on my podcast, *Heart of the Story*, along with bonus material, such as accompanying meditations and stories of the inspiration behind each essay.

Other episodes not listed here contain healing meditations, life lessons, and interviews with female creatives and seekers. You can find versions of select chapters on the following podcast episodes.

SECTION 1: LOOKING WITHIN

Chapter 1: Your Inner Sage	Ep. 1 "How to Harness Your Inner Wisdom When Everything Feels Uncertain"
Chapter 2: Somebody, Someday	Ep. 2 "You Have Permission"
Chapter 3: Put the Paintbrush Down	Ep. 4 "You Don't Have to Be Perfect"
Chapter 4: Loosen the Edges	Ep. 22 "You Are Worthy"
Chapter 5: Pay It Forward	Ep. 9 "How Unexpected Generosity Changed My Life"
Chapter 6: Again	Ep. 65 "Holding Onto the Moment"
Chapter 7: Remember Today	Ep. 3 "How to Have Hope"

SECTION 2: LEARNING AND EXPANDING

Chapter 8: Triage   Ep. 15 "Prioritizing Time with Yourself"

Chapter 11: Nature Lessons   Ep. 33 "Living Seasonally" and
                                         Ep. 56 "Seasonal Living: Spring"

Chapter 13: Trampoline Savasana   Ep. 14 "Creating Meaningful Rituals"

Chapter 14: Noticing Walks   Ep. 13 "How to Truly See Yourself"

SECTION 3: DEALING AND HEALING WHEN LIFE DOESN'T GO AS PLANNED

Chapter 15: Fierce   Ep. 46 "You Are Fierce"

Chapter 16: Joy in Hidden Places   Ep. 8 "Finding Joy in Hidden Places"

Chapter 17: Puzzle Pieces   Ep. 42 "Trading Busy for a Beautiful Life"

Chapter 18: The Last First Snowfall   Ep. 40 "How to Get Closure"

Chapter 20: The Opposite of Loss   Ep. 62 "Healing When Your Heart Is Hurting"

Chapter 21: You Are Welcome Here   Ep. 11 "You Are Never Alone"

SECTION 4: CHARTING A NEW COURSE

Chapter 22: The Hum of Your Heart   Ep. 54 "What Your Heart Really Yearns For"

Chapter 23: Coyotes   Ep. 38 "Nurturing Your Nervous System"

Chapter 24: Finding New Shells   Ep. 23 "Remaking Your Life"

Chapter 26: Walks in the Woods   Ep. 53 "All About Love"

Chapter 27: If You Want to Know Who I Am   Ep. 72 "My Summer Travels"

References

Angelou, Maya. 2013. *Mom & Me & Mom*. New York, Random House Large Print.

OWN: SuperSoul Sessions. "Rob Bell: Is Your Best Day Behind You?" *Oprah* video. 1:12, Dec 11, 2015. https://www.oprah.com/own-supersoulsessions/rob-bell-on-what-his-most-powerful-prayers-sound-like.

Sia, "Bird Set Free," 2016, Track 1 on *This Is Acting*, Monkey Puzzle: RCA, 2016, Digital.

Oliver, Mary. 1986. *Dream Work*. Boston, Atlantic Monthly Press.

Doyle, Glennon. 2020. *Untamed* First edition. The Dial Press.

Schildkret, Day. 2022. *Hello, Goodbye*. S&S/Simon Element.

Niequist, Shauna. 2016. *Present Over Perfect*. Zondervan.

Stanley, Tracee. 2021. *Radiant Rest*. Shambhala Publications.

Trudeau, Renée. 2022. "Ready to Prioritize Your Self-Care? Start Here." *Self-Care* (blog). November 7, 2022. https://reneetrudeau.com/2022/11/ready-to-prioritize-your-self-care-start-here/

McBride, Hillary. 2021. *The Wisdom of Your Body*. Brazos Press.

Gilbert, Elizabeth. 2014. "Thought of the Day: Don't Live Somebody Else's Dream." *Thought of the Day* (blog). November 1, 2014. https://www.elizabethgilbert.com/thought-of-the-day-dont-live-somebody-elses-dream-dear-ones-i-found-this/

Acknowledgments

Thank you, dear readers, for being vulnerable enough to pick up this book and go on a heart journey with me.

My sincerest thanks to my spiritual mentor, Ann Baker, who taught me a completely different way to live—the way of my heart. Thank you to my other mentors—Shauna Niequist, Leeana Tankersely, Maya Angelou, Glennon Doyle, Elizabeth Gilbert, Martha Beck, Sarah Blondin, Tracee Stanley, and Mary Oliver. Reading your books has helped me remember that home is in my soul.

Much of my heart work has happened with amazing retreat leaders at incredible wellness centers—Elizabeth Gilbert and Cheryl Strayed at 1440 Multiversity, Renée Trudeau at Kripalu, Flora Bowley at Omega, Patty McNair at Ragdale, the amazing people at Esalen, and the organizers of the San Miguel Writer's Conference.

Thank you, Heidi Rose Robbins, for connecting me with this publishing house. Thank you to Lindsey, Lucy, and Andrew for bringing my book to life.

Thank you to the artist residency centers that supported the writing of this book—Ragdale and Write on Door County. Thank you for giving writers the time and space to create.

Many of these essays originally appeared on my podcast *Heart of the Story* and were produced by my uber-talented producer, Michelle Redo. Thank you for completely "getting" me and bringing my vision to life. And thank you to all of the incredible guests that have graced the podcast.

In the spring of 2020, when the world was shut down, I decided that creativity would not be shut down, and my Writer Workout community was born. Meeting with you every Monday is one of my greatest joys in life.

In memory of my father, who passed in April 2021. I hope you're driving on a winding beach road in a red Mustang with the top down on your way to go deep sea fishing. Thank you for visiting me during many journal sessions. May these words be a window into my soul.

To my mom and sister, thank you for being there, always—for laughs, adventures, and the hard times. I know that you'd do anything for me.

My deepest love to my boys. I never knew we'd be accidental wanderers, and yet, you've made every place home. Lover, your cooking and love and presence nurture me, heart and soul. Boo Bear, you are an absolute miracle. Every time I look at you, my mama heart melts with the deepest contentment and gratitude. How did I get so lucky?

About the Author

Award-winning author Nadine Kenney Johnstone is a holistic writing coach who helps women develop and publish their stories. Her articles and interviews have appeared in *Cosmo, Authority, MindBodyGreen, HERE, Urban Wellness, Natural Awakenings, Yogi Approved*, and more. Nadine is the podcast host of *Heart of the Story*, where she shares stories from the heart and interviews with today's most impactful female creatives. Pulling from her vast experience as a writing, meditation, and yoga nidra instructor, Nadine leads women's workshops and retreats online and around the U.S.

nadinekenneyjohnstone.com
IG: nadinekenneyjohnstone

AN INVITATION

If you'd like guidance and support with your inner exploration, my soul-replenishment retreats for women offer a nurturing environment for coming home to your heart. You can find out more at: https://nadinekenneyjohnstone.com/well-retreats.

www.ingramcontent.com/pod-product-compliance
Lightning Source LLC
Chambersburg PA
CBHW061406010526
44119CB00011B/274